Jonathan Tenney

New England in Albany

Jonathan Tenney

New England in Albany

ISBN/EAN: 9783741123764

Manufactured in Europe, USA, Canada, Australia, Japa

Cover: Foto ©Lupo / pixelio.de

Manufactured and distributed by brebook publishing software
(www.brebook.com)

NEW ENGLAND

IN ALBANY.

BY JONATHAN TENNEY, A. M.

BOSTON:

CROCKER & CO., PUBLISHERS.

1883.

NEW ENGLAND IN ALBANY.

ALBANY AS BEAVERWYCK AND RENSSELAER-WYCK.

Albany is one of the oldest settled towns in the United States. St. Augustine settled in 1565; Jamestown in 1607; New York in 1612; and Plymouth in 1620, are older. When Hudson in 1609 passed up the river which bears his name, he may have passed the territory now called Albany; but he made no settlement. Shortly after, Adrian Block and some other Dutch adventurers followed in the track of Hudson, and discovered how readily and profitably the trade in furs could be carried on with the Indians along the coasts and up the rivers. In 1614, the United New Netherlands Company, under grant from the States General of Holland, established a trading house and fortified it with guns and twelve men in Castle Island, four miles below the present site of Albany. They named their fort Nassau. The spring floods and ice injuring their works, they afterwards removed them to higher ground near by. For four years they pursued a lucrative trade with the natives, purchasing their furs for trinkets and finding a ready market. At the end of this time their Charter having expired, the States declined, for some reason now unknown, to renew it. But a Charter with almost unlimited powers as to jurisdiction, colonization, erecting forts, and trade, was given to a company of wealthy

Dutch merchants, called the West India Company, in June 1621. This Company erected a fort on the present site of Albany in 1623, and named it Fort Orange. Thus was commenced the settlement of Beaverwyck, now Albany. The fort was manned, and a few Dutch traders huddled in their shanties close around it, for the purpose of carrying on the fur trade with the Indians.

On account of the slow growth of the colony of New Netherlands, the States were induced, in 1629, to pass an ordinance, granting to any member of the Company, the right of selecting any tract of land, outside of the island of Manhattan, sixteen miles on one side, or eight miles on either side, of any navigable stream, and extending as far inland as the patroon, as the proprietor was called, should choose. The chief conditions imposed were the establishment of a colony of at least fifty persons over fifteen years of age, on said tract, within four years, the payment of five per cent. on all trade except that of furs, which the States reserved to itself. The patroon and settlers were precluded from any voice in the government of the colony, and from any manufacture of cloth; but this feudal lord, as he might be called, had full power over the lands of his tenants. All necessary local officers were appointed by him, and unrestricted privileges of hunting, fowling, and fishing given him.

Under these grants, Kilian Van Rensselaer, a director of the Company, a pearl and diamond merchant, secured, with additional purchases made through his agents, land twenty-four miles each side the Hudson, and forty-eight miles inland, constituting Rensselaerwyck, and including what is now Albany county, most of Rensselaer county, and a part of the county of Columbia. The first colony came over in 1630 and

Jonathan Tenney

New England in Albany

settled near Fort Orange. This fort, with its limited sur-
roundings was not under the patroon.

Manhattan, now New York, was the residence of the colo-
nial governor. This with Beaverwyck and Rensselaerwyck,
was all that constituted the province of New Netherlands at
that time.

The cruel wars with the Indians at Manhattan stirred up
and kept up by the testy Kieft, did not disturb the settlers
about Fort Orange. They had been cordially welcomed by
the Iroquois, with whom, in solemn council, they early made
a firm and lasting treaty. The Dutchman came neither
for agriculture, nor for conquest of territory, but for furs and
peltry. It was his policy to keep peace and make gain.
The five nations, including the Mohawks, Oneidas, Onon-
dagas, Cayugas and Senecas, called collectively the Iroquois,
possessed nearly all of the present state of New York, west
of the Hudson, except a portion near the island of Manhattan.
This was occupied by another tribe. When the Dutch
arrived here, the Iroquois were at war with the Algonquins,
or Canada Indians, who had formed an alliance with the
French. Right glad were they to ally themselves with
another European nation that knew how to use the terrible
enginery of powder and guns. So, with this notion of self-
protection, united with their natural love for trinkets and
strong drink, it was easy to keep them on terms of peace and
submission. The treaty was mutually advantageous for long
years. It brought peace to the Indians and plenty to the
Dutchman.

People of all nations were admitted to this settlement, pro-
vided they had license from the provincial governor at New
York and conformed to the regulations of the Company and

the patroon. And yet Beaverwyck contained only ten houses in 1646. A few small farms had been taken up near by; a brewery had been erected by the patroon in 1637; some few small mills for sawing and grinding for immediate use were carried by the wind, by horses, or by the waters of the creeks. Still, fur trading was the great business, which no local difficulty, no alarms of war elsewhere disturbed. The annual trade at this time has been estimated at about 16,000 beavers.

The settlers had little care for learning or religion. only for the liberty of trade. The Reformed Dutch Church was established by law, and an oath to support the government of Holland was required. The first clergyman that appeared in Beaverwyck, came in 1642, and a schoolmaster at the same time. A small church was soon erected; nine benches seated the audience. But we have no record of the labors or influence of those public teachers. They were sent, not called for.

The fruits of the earth were abundant and cheaply procured, so that agriculture received but little attention. The Indians brought corn and beans cultivated by the squaws. While the province was under the administration of the honest-hearted but head-strong Peter Stuyvesant, from 1646 to 1664, there was much contention of words between the governor and the officers of the patroon as to certain privileges and jurisdiction. These led even to violence and imprisonments. There was, also, besides the Indian hostilities, some strife between the colonists in Connecticut and the Provincial government at Manhattan. Yet, matters as to the fur trade at Beaverwyck were but little disturbed.

ALBANY AFTER THE ENGLISH CONQUEST.

The Province of New Netherlands was easily wrested from the hands of the Dutch under Stuyvesant in 1664, by the English, who had always claimed it as their territory. Manhattan became New York and Beaverwyck became Albany. These lands had been granted by Charles II to his brother the Duke of York and Albany, afterwards James II. He made his claim good without bloodshed. For a little over a hundred years, until the Revolution of 1776, it remained under the English rule, with the exception of a few months in 1673-4.

While changes were made in governors and in some of the forms of goverment, it was many years before those changes disturbed essentially the settlement at Albany. The governors were usually of short reign; some popular, and some unpopular. But they were generally so engaged in wars with French and Indians, and in petty schemes of their own, or of the English crown, that there was little interference with the trading and pursuits of this northern town. Albany became a city in 1686. In 1698, it had a population of only 803, among which there were only five English families and one Scotch family. The rest were still Dutch. The English required them to pay their taxes and obey the government. This they did. They were secure in all the possessions they owned, and in their religious and family relations. They had as little as possible to do with politics or war. With great sagacity they managed to keep the Indians on terms of friendship, and to command all their trade. This trade was as extensive as the hunting grounds of the five nations, then covering nearly all of the present state of New York.

In course of time, especially through the influence of the patroon, agriculture increased, and there was a surplus of wheat and peas. Timber was prepared for the market. A few of the settlers made a profitable trade with New York City in these commodities; but Albany was not a great agricultural region. The fur trade with the Indians was the great business just as long as furs could be collected. They could be bought cheap and yielded a large profit. Agriculture and manufactures, education and religion, the wars of the nations, and the affairs of courts were of little interest to these traders.

NEW NETHERLANDS AND NEW ENGLAND.

The Puritans of New England and the Dutch of New Netherlands had met before they met in the wilds of North America. Not satisfied with the ritualism of the Church of England, a band of English Puritans had gone over to Holland early in the 17th century, and there formed a church after their own model. The Dutch Reformed Church was essentially Calvinistic; so was the English Church of the good pastor, John Robinson. The Hollanders were tolerant; the Puritans were industrious and law abiding. So they got on well together. Yet, after a twelve years' residence, the Puritan was not sufficiently pleased with that country to make it his permanent home. There was a disagreeable element in the Dutch that did not suit the English. The Englishman was a diligent farmer, the Dutchman a greedy trader; the Englishman was seeking for "more light," the Dutchman was satisfied with what light he had. The Puritan felt that he was only a "pilgrim and a stranger" in Holland, a country where he could not train his children as he would, in which he could not pursue his vocation as he would; and, above all in which he could not enjoy the largest religious liberty.

Our "Pilgrim Fathers" came to wild New England where they at once laid the foundation of "a church without a bishop, and a state without a king." They established free schools for their children, and taught them lessons in industry, frugality, freedom, and piety.

Our Dutch fathers came about the same time to the beautiful banks of the Hudson, and pursued the lucrative fur trade with the Indians. The school and the church gave them no concern. The government was left with rapacious and arbitrary governors.

About 1627, Gov. Bradford, hearing that the Dutch were at the mouth of the Hudson, and encroaching upon his territory by sending ships to Narragansett Bay to trade, sent Mr. Winslow to remonstrate. The vessel had sailed away before his arrrival. Soon after this, Gov. Minuit of Manhattan, sent a very friendly letter to Gov. Bradford, congratulating Plymouth Colony upon its prosperity, and proposing trade and friendly relations in the future. To this the Governor of Plymouth replied in the most friendly terms, alluding to the hospitality which the Pilgrims had received in Holland, and assuring the Governor of New Netherlands that they and their children after them would never forget the same. At the same time he assured Gov. Minuit, that he must respect the rightful claim of the Pilgrims and not allow his skiffs to come to Narragansett for beavers. He also complained that the Dutch were selling muskets, powder and shot to the Indians. Other courtesies of the most pleasing character were kept up during the time of Minuit, in which, while each decidedly claimed what he regarded as territorial right, there arose no unfriendly words or conduct.

It is said that the Dutch invited the New Englanders to come to the rich and fertile valley of the Connecticut River, and that, in turn, the New Englanders advised the Dutch to make good their claim to the banks of the Hudson.

But this pleasant state of things did not continue under the rapacious Von Twiller, the testy Kieft, or the honest but headstrong Stuyvesant. Kings and States in chartered gifts, had got matters strangely mixed. England and Holland had both given away the same territory when it belonged to neither. It was the home of the aboriginal Indian.

The New Englander pushed his way into the valley of Connecticut and all along the coasts and plains of Long Island without asking the New Netherlander, and even in defiance of his attempts to hinder, when he saw how aggressive the " Pilgrim " was inclined to be. The charter, the Indian title, and the divine right and duty of cultivating all good corn land, furnished his justification.

In 1643, things had come to such a pass that the colonies of Massachusetts, Connecticut and New Haven, formed a union called the United Colonies of New England. Its purposes were to protect themselves against the Indians and against the encroachments of the Dutch. The population of New England was then about 20,000, while that of New Netherlands was only about 1,000. The English claim was based on the prior discovery of North America by Cabot, while the Dutch claim was based on the special discovery of Hudson and prior occupancy.

THE HOLLANDER AND THE NEW ENGLANDER UNDER THE ENGLISH.

These claims and consequent occupation by the English settlers of New England, led to much bitter controversy.

It was partially but never fully settled until the forced surrender, in 1664, of New Amsterdam, and finally, of all the Dutch claims in North America, to the English under Charles II. who had given all this territory to his brother, the Duke of York and Albany.

Might made right. It is not now our province to discuss the question of natural or acquired right at that time. But certain it is, that the restless New Englander, pushing his way with his bold self assertion, his indomitable energy, and his intense love of individual freedom of thought and expression, had forced himself into the New Netherlands, and made himself felt in its government, so that the wise, good and inflexible Peter Stuyvesant, the last of the Dutch Governors, saw himself compelled to yield his authority or fight and do worse. New Amsterdam became New York, Beaverwyck became Albany; and this without bloodshed. This was the first New England in Albany.

But this was not fully accomplished. The world moved slowly then; but it moved. Years of thought and discussion. of doing and enduring. had yet to come. More than a century of war and blood; of life and death; of toil and struggle. before we were the United States of America.

The English crown did not readily yield to the claims of the people. nor were the people quite ready to sever themselves from their mother England. The autocracy of Great Britain had not done their greatest folly in tyrannizing over the land of nobles in peasant garb. These nobles were right. and were growing mighty. They endured and waited; thought and discussed. It was so in New England and Virginia.

Meanwhile, the Dutch, the Scotch, the Irish, the Swede

and the Huguenot were looking on and learning. A day was to come when they would all see alike, and become one great people.

The money-loving Hollander was little disturbed by the changes that were going on. It was especially so at Albany. He had had little to do with the government. He was up the river 150 miles, and things in the New Amsterdam that was, were done before he knew it. The new English government told him he would not be disturbed in his gainful trade, if he would take the oath of allegiance and respect the English officers. He accepted the situation and made good bargains as before.

He, somehow, didn't like the Yankee, and the Yankee didn't like him. Few of them came to Albany until after the Revolution. There was a mutual repulsion. One hundred years later, a common cause, common needs, feelings and struggles brought them to know each other. Then the sons of the Hollander and of the English Pilgrim of the early part of the 17th century became friends again, as they are now.

ALBANY AND NEW ENGLAND DURING THE ENGLISH AND FRENCH WARS.

But as to the wars. In 1690, New England had over 200,000 people within its borders. There were settlements all over it. The State of New York was limited to settlements on the Hudson, a little way up the Mohawk, and on Long Island. Then came King William's war, (1690-97) between France and England. Schenectady was burned. The New England settlers suffered the most direful atrocities from the Indians.

The brave Col. Schuyler of Albany did some service in that war. But Albany was fortified and palisadoed, and its citizens stayed safely at home, while Massachusetts and Connecticut did the fighting and enduring to protect them. Queen Anne's war came (1702-13) ; and while blood flowed in nearly every village in Massachusetts and New Hampshire, the peace of Albany was not disturbed.

In the war between England and France, (1744-48) when the strongly fortified Louisburg fell by New England arms, Albany had but little to do, nothing to suffer, except it may be from the heavy debt that came upon the colonies after it was over.

It was in the " French War " (1754-60) that France lost all its possessions in North America. Sir Wm. Johnson was in the service, and writes, in 1755, of "great opposition from the Dutch traders at Albany," and adds, "by their cabals and weight in the assembly may perhaps distress"; "those people are so devoted to their own private profit that every other publick principle has ever been sacrificed to it." The fighting in that war was mostly done by New England. The city of Albany was making money by furnishing supplies.

ALBANY IN THE REVOLUTION.

There was held at Albany, as a central place, in June 1754, a Provincial Congress. It was not large ; but its deliberations looking to a union of the colonies and securing the Indian friendship and aid, were wise and had great lasting results.

Among those present were Theodore Atkinson of New Hampshire, Thomas Hutchinson of Massachusetts, and that common-sense patriot Benjamin Franklin of Boston, repre-

senting Pennsylvania. They were among the early New
Englanders in Albany.

The people of the Hudson and Mohawk valleys were very
slow to unite with the New England, Virginia, and other
colonies against British aggression prior to the revolution of
1776. The battle of Lexington aroused the city of New
York, and the more patriotic and far seeing in Albany. The
Van Rensselaers, Schuylers, Gansevoort, and a few other
leading men of Holland descent, nobly gave their money and
their service to the cause of their oppressed countrymen.
But the Dutch generally were apathetic. They preferred the
peaceful and profitable pursuits of traffic to the expensive and
hazardous contests of a war for independence. On this point
Bancroft, Lossing, and other historic writers are authority.

Albany was fortified and garrisoned. Its inhabitants lived
in a village fenced by palisades. It had gates guarded by a
watch; and block houses. Loaded arms were kept by the
citizens in their houses, in their stores, and in church. Scouts
were on the lookout for approach of danger. They were well
defended. They were never attacked nor beleaguered. They
complained when soldiers were billetted upon them and when
impressments were made. But they were delighted with the
trade they brought them, the lively society they made, and the
protection they gave. All historians agree that tories were
numerous hereabouts.

Gen. John Stark, who was, for some time, in command of
the Northern Department of the Army of the Revolution,
having his headquarters at Albany, was on the most cordial
terms with Gen. Schuyler and other patriots of the city. In
1781, he writes to Gov. Clinton, "I am fully confident that
George the III. of Great Britain, has many subjects in this

city who would willingly lay down half, nay, even the whole
of their estates in his service, and trust in his royal clemency
for the re-payment of the money so profitably laid out."
Again, "Albany is a very dangerous place to put men into."
Again, "I have no hopes of any assistance from Albany; it
is not their inclination to fight away from their own castle."
The battles of the Revolution were chiefly fought by the
men of New England. It was so not only at Lexington
and Bunker Hill and Bennington; it was so at Saratoga and
Trenton, and all through the war that sustained the Declara-
tion of Independence and gave us a nation of freemen. They
did it under such leaders as Allen and Warner of Vermont;
Bedell, Rogers, Poor, Stark, and Sullivan of New Hampshire;
Warren, Knox, Prescott, Lyman, Thomas, Winslow, Lincoln,
Heath and Williams of Massachusetts; Wooster, Knowlton,
Putnam and Arnold of Connecticut, and Greene of Rhode
Island, — not forgetting some brave coadjutors from New
York and other Colonies.

These statements are due to the truth of history. Until the
final adoption of the constitution of 1787, the sympathies and
hearty co-operation of the Dutch people of New York, with
a few noble exceptions, were not with the English speaking
people of the other colonies, in the contest for freedom and a
United Government of the States. But when it was accomplished, they became law abiding, wealth producing citizens.
Such was their nature. The Union to-day, and the State of
New York, in particular, have reason to be glad in the powerful influence which the domestic and social virtues, the
indomitable patience and perseverance, simple manners, and
steady habits of the early Dutch settlers did have and are
still having, upon the moral and civil institutions of the

country. Virginia, New York and Massachusetts are now one; welded together by common struggles and common triumphs; common blood and common interests. The patriot graves and historic monuments of great deeds are one. The treasures of history and of industry are one. The great past and the vast future belong to us all.

NEW ENGLANDERS IN ALBANY.

I find no certain evidence that any New Englanders came to Albany for permanent settlement prior to the Revolution of 1776. They were to be found in New York City, and in some of the lower counties, earlier than this date. In a list of the heads of families in the city in 1697, five are reported as English in a population of 803; but these were probably direct from England. There were English soldiers and officers in the fort at that time. The Society for the Propagation of the Gospel in Foreign Parts sent missionaries here, who preached to the people and made some efforts to christianize the Indians. There were English chaplains here. An English Episcopal Church was erected near the fort, in State street, in 1716, the services in which were attended by the garrison and a very few residents.

Soon after the close of the French war in 1763, a Presbyterian church was formed, the attendants upon which were, at first, mostly Scotch, with a few English.

The war of the Revolution opened the way to the State of New York for the New Englander. He had been there during the wars, and saw rich lands, vast forests, and fine products. It was a field for adventure and enterprise open to his active nature. New England farmers were poor. The long wars had made them so. The boys must do something. Said a Connecticut farmer to his son,—" My son, here is a horse ; it is all I can give you ; take it and go." He came to Albany, opened a tavern, and became a wealthy and influential citizen. Usually these emigrants to "York State" were tillers of the soil, with a few mechanics and traders. Westward the stream of population ran. Albany was the route through which they took their line of march, usually going beyond any settlements into the wilderness. They feared nothing but the savages. The Yankee, John Sullivan, and the treaty which soon followed had reduced them to quiet. Some stopped in Oneida, some in Montgomery, some in Madison, and some in Onondaga; others pushed their way on to the Genesee Valley, sending out branch colonies to the northern and southern parts of the state ; filling, in time, nearly the whole territory west of the Hudson, except the small section occupied by the Dutch on the Hudson and Mohawk, and by the Germans of Herkimer County. And here now live their descendants. Volumes could not tell what they have done in this 19th. century, and how they did it. They can only say, look around you and behold ! They came ; they saw ; they conquered.

But we are writing about Albany. That there were very few in Albany who spoke the English tongue, and, hence, few New Englanders previous to about 1790, is evidenced by the testimony of Dr. William Bay, son of Rev. Andrew Bay, who was pastor of the first Presbyterian church some years on from 1765. Dr. Bay was born in Albany, Oct. 14, 1773, educated at Columbia College, and spent a long professional life here. He states that the population was so essentially Dutch in his boyhood, that but few of his mates could speak any other than the Dutch language. Rev. Mr. Rogers, in his

History of the Reformed Church in Albany, observes that the Rev. Dr. Westerlo, of that church, "in 1782, began to preach half the day in English."

There are few living now who are authority in regard to the nativity of the families who came to this city prior to 1800. Death and removal have left many of them without descendants here to-day. In other cases, no family records dating so far back have been kept. We have spent much time in research as to this matter, and give the best results we can up to this writing. We have resorted to imperfectly kept church records, records of tomb-stones, and to the newspapers of the time. Munsell's Annals' have contributed their aid. Tradition of the older and more observing citizens has given its often unsatisfactory help. All these have been compared and reduced to probability; in most cases, we trust, to certainty; but a certainty far too incomplete. And, yet, enough is presented, we think, to show when, why, and in what manner the elements of New England civilization were introduced into Albany, and finally, commingling with all that is peculiarly worthy in the Dutch, with a share of English, Scotch, German, Irish, French, Huguenot, and Hebrew, and a sprinkling of other nationalities, have at length, become so modified and assimilated by intermarriages, social and business intercourse, and the refining influences of religious and intellectual culture, that there are now few, if any, cities in our union that can exhibit to-day, as a result of all these, a state of society more homogeneous, harmonious, healthy, intelligent, and moral, than this city of Albany.

Among the emigrants from New England making their way westward for home and fortune, many, of a trading turn, saw the natural advantages of Albany, and went no further.

Others tarried here and opened the genuine "traveler's home," a New England tavern. The most important of these, for many years, were kept almost exclusively by Yankees. Still others remained to pursue the various mechanic arts demanded at that time. Nearly all "came to stay," and were successful. Then soon followed the school-master, the doctor, the lawyer, and now and then a clergyman.

The tide of emigration was astonishing to the old inhabitants. Says a letter written from Otsego County, in 1789: "The vast multitudes of people that come daily to this country have caused a scarcity of provisions amounting almost to a famine. In Genesee it is quite so; corn will bring ten shillings there in cash, and six shillings in Albany; and it is said that potatoes at Niagara are twenty shillings. However alarming this may be, it proceeds from no other cause than that of an innumerable quantity of people flocking in. I have had 30 in a day seeking land of me." Says another; "Complaints were frequent at that time of the scarcity of provisions in the western part of the state on account of the flood of immigrants. In the vicinity of Niagara, it was difficult to subsist the new comers." But these "new comers" went to work on their fertile farms, and soon had enough and to spare. Bread stuffs were sent on in plenty for the Albany, New York, and Boston trade. So industrious, frugal, and enterprising were they.

Says a local paper in June, 1791 :—"Motley processions of eastern emigrants are daily passing through the city. Albany is the grand thoroughfare to the western country. The "Far West" of these New Englanders, as they mostly are, is the Genesee Valley; and they are accompanied by their families, their flocks, and their implements."

A treaty of peace and amity was made at Canandaigua, in 1794, between the United States and the Six Nations. The fear of danger from Indian depredations was removed. The Genesee Valley immediately became the El Dorado to the stirring people of the eastern states. More than before went on the "moving to York State."

Says another writer concerning the farm-lands of Albany County, with which the Dutch had done but little in all those years since 1623, "The settlements on these lands did not increase very rapidly until the Yankees poured in about 1794."

It may be remarked that some of the best citizens of the country towns about Albany to-day are descendants of these Yankees.

It is written that a citizen of Albany on the 28th of February, 1795, took a count of that day's travel through the city, and enumerated five hundred sleighs from sunrise to sunset. Another estimated, near that time, that about twelve hundred sleighs freighted with men, women, children and furniture had passed through the city from the east within three successive days. It was a phenomenon to the quiet burghers of the staid old town ; and many wondered if New England was being depopulated. But its sons, and daughters, too, have been going "out west," and even south, ever since, so that they are known by their works, in every state, territory, and city in the land. Yet New England is full of busy, populous cities ; and its villages and rural districts are dotted with pleasant, intelligent, and virtuous homes, made thrifty by industry and economy.

In 1800, Albany, although it had been settled over 175 years, and been a city 114 years, and occupied a commanding position as the capital of the state and as a commercial center, was a small town. Its population was only 5,387, showing an increase of nearly 2,000 since 1790. "The face of nature around it had been but little disturbed," says Mr. Worth, who came to Albany as a banker, about 1801, in his "Recollections of Albany." Old as it was, it still retained its primitive aspect, and still stood in all its original simplicity; maintaining its quaint and quiescent character, unchanged, unmodified, unimproved; still particularly adhering, in all its walks, to the old track. The rude hand of innovation, however, was then just beginning to be felt; and slight as was the touch, it was felt as an injury, or resented as an insult. * * "All was antique, clean, and quiet." * * "No noise, no hurry, no confusion." "No putting up, nor pulling down; no ill-looking excavations, no leveling of hills, no filling up of valleys; in short, none of those villainous improvements which disfigure the face of nature, and exhibit the restless spirit of the Anglo-Saxon race." The stinted pines still covered the hills to the very edge of the city, and the ravines and valleys were clothed with evergreens, intermixed with briars and spangled with wild rose." "The little islands below the town were feathered with foliage down to the very water's edge, and bordered with stately trees." "As far as the eye could extend up and down the river, all remained comparatively wild and beautiful." "Pearl street, was, in those days, the west end of the town." "There resided some of the most aristocratic of the ancient burghers." The accumulated profits of trade, united with the simplest habits and rigid economy, for nearly two centuries had made the Dutch of Albany, even at that day, rich; and riches, where money is the main thing, makes an aristocracy in any town. Aristocracy gives dignity of bearing and retirement from business. Our

graphic writer goes on :—" There, a little after sunrise, in a
mild morning, might be seen, sitting by the side of their doors,"
(every Dutch house has a stoop), " the ancient and venerable
mynheers with their little sharp cocked hats, and red-ringed
worsted caps, drawn tightly over their heads. There they
sat, like monuments of a former age, smoking their pipes in
dignified silence and with phlegmatic gravity. The whole
line of the street, on either side, was dotted by the little
clouds of smoke that, issuing from their pipes, and curling
round their noddles, rose slowly up the antique gables, and
mingled with the morning air, giving beauty to the scene, and
adding an air of life to the picture." " Albany was indeed
Dutch, in all its moods and tenses, thoroughly and inveterately
Dutch. The buildings were Dutch, — Dutch in style, in
position, attitude and aspect. The people were Dutch, the
houses were Dutch, and even the dogs were Dutch. If any
confirmation were wanting as to the origin and character of
the place, it might be found in the old Dutch church, which
was itself always to be found in the middle of State street,
looking as if it had been wheeled out of line by the giants of
old and there left, or had dropped down from the clouds in a
dark night and had stuck fast where it fell." "All the old
buildings in the city,—and they constituted a majority,—were
but one story high, with sharp peaked roofs, surmounted by a
rooster, vulgarly called a weathercock. Every house having
any pretensions to dignity was placed with its gable-end to
the street, and was ornamented with huge iron numericals,
announcing the date of its erection ; while from its eaves hung
wooden gutters or spouts, projected in front some six or seven
feet, so as to discharge the water from the roof when it rained,
directly over the center of the side walks." " But the destined

hour was drawing near. The Yankees were creeping in. Every day added to their number; and the unhallowed hand of innovation was seen pointing its impertinent finger at the cherished habits and venerated customs of the ancient burghers. These meddling Eastern Saxons had, at length, obtained a majority in the city councils."

After speaking of some of the innovations commenced, and the manner of treating some of the leaders in them by the native inhabitants, Mr. Worth goes on to say:—"This done, they went to sleep again; and before they awoke new swarms had arrived, and a complete and thorough revolution had taken place. The Yankees had taken possession of the city, and the fate of the Dutch was sealed."

"A restless, leveling, innovating spirit now prevailed throughout the city. The detested word *"improvement"* was in every mouth, and resistance was unavailing. The stinted pines became alarmed and gradually receded. The hills themselves gave way; new streets opened their extended lines, and the old ones grew wider. The roosters in the gable-heads, * * * now gave it up, and came quietly down. The gables in despair soon followed, and more imposing fronts soon raised their corniced heads. The old Dutch church itself * * * submitted to its fate and fell * * * at the foot of State street, which freed from that obstruction, thence forward became the Rialto of the city, where peddlers * * * and country hucksters now do congregate."

"Even the dogs began to bark in broken English; many of them had, indeed, already caught the Yankee twang, so rapid was the progress of refinement. In the process of a few brief years, all that was venerable in the eyes of the ancient burghers disappeared." "It is hardly necessary to say that not an iron rooster has crowed upon the gable-heads, nor a civil cocked hat been seen in the ancient city of Albany from that day to this."

The ancient Dutch families, many of them, although wealthy and respectable, were never the most enterprising. The wealth of traffic, in the first one hundred and fifty years, had been poured into the laps of their ancestors while they looked on, gathered and hoarded. Now an equally greedy and more active people had entered upon the opportunities of the situation. Here they frequently, after confidence had been gained, induced the original citizen to show his money and invest it in active trade. Here, too, it often happened that he made himself a member of these old families by making an amiable and frugal daughter his partner for life. Then the large estates were divided and made to produce incomes by the toils and profits of new kinds of traffic, carried on in a new way and by a new people. The growth of Albany, as compared with more recent cities in our country, has always been slow: but it has been sure. The great West down to about 1810, was little but a vast wilderness, tenanted by wild beasts and the wilder aborigines. These same descendants of the ever-moving, unyielding, all-conquering, Anglo-Saxon race, have possessed this vast western territory and made it a fruitful field, all full of villages and peoples of productive industry. Albany, from its advantageous position, has derived wealth and growth from western trade. It is not our purpose now to discuss how much more it might have done with greater enterprise and foresight. The city has been growing, we repeat, since 1800; growing slowly but surely. But it has grown because the West has grown. The settlers that came from the eastern states, about that time and since, with their descendants, have seized their opportunities and put wisdom and energy into them. The state of feeling that had existed on account of conflicting interests as to territory and trade between the Dutch and the New Englanders, ever since the days of Peter Stuyvesant, had become somewhat modified by the mutual sufferings and interests of the French wars, and more by the war of the Revolution. But still, among the masses especially, there was some of the old jealousy and prejudice remaining after the Revolution, and even down to about the date of the opening of the Erie Canal, perhaps later. The disappearance has been gradual as generations have passed away. Now history tells its story without jealousy or prejudice,—simply as truth,—just as it tells of the Salem Witchcraft, the Negro Plot of New York City, and the persecutions which our ancestors in common, in that dark day, inflicted upon Quakers and Baptists in New England, and upon the Waldenses and Lutherans in New York. Elements that were once antago-nistic to each other in this city, and thus hindered progress in art, commerce. manufactures, education and religion, now united, are all strongly pressing on for their advancement.

Among the New Englanders who went no farther west, but stopped on the banks of the Hudson and finally made Albany their home during a part, and in many instances, the whole of their lives. we first mention those who came about the time of the Revolution of 1776 and onward to about the beginning of this century. They were the pioneers in this new coloniza-tion of Albany and vicinity. They laid the foundations. We are sorry that we have no sources from which we can draw to make this list complete. In a few instances. indeed, we allow strong probability to take the place of fact, as to whether certain men of pure English names came directly from England, or had first received their training in that rock-bound, sea-environed land of free schools and rough discipline of toil and struggle—New England. It is certain that some who came here early from Long Island, New York City, Orange, Putnam, Columbia, Dutchess, Schoharie, Montgomery, Saratoga, and Rensselaer counties, were of New England parentage. All such are properly classed as New Englanders.

It is worthy of the note made of it by a close observer of that time, that there was a great number of aged people of Holland ancestry at the beginning of this century who had retired from the pursuit of gain and were quietly passing away just as the "new comers," with their new ideas and habits, were ready to step into their places. "The population of the city was evidently undergoing a revolution." One generation went away; another entirely different came in its place.

New England settlers in Albany between about 1780 and 1800, were as follows, as nearly as can be ascertained:

Solomon Allen, hatter.

Ezra Ames, painter.

Thomas Andrews.

Eleazer F. Backus, bookseller.

Benjamin Baker.

John Blake, stage proprietor.

Christopher Batterman, builder.

Moses Beal, stage proprietor.

William P. Beers, merchant.

Abraham Bloodgood, trader.

Francis Bloodgood, merchant.

James Bloodgood, merchant.

26, 1846; gr. Williams, 1866, and M. D. at Albany and Columbia, 1870; lecturer at Albany Med. Col.; has been del. to Am. Med. Ass. and N. Y. Med. Soc.; prest. Albany Co. Med. Soc.; prest. Y. M. A.; and is an active, successful, rising physician and citizen.

Capt. Abraham Bloodgood is first mentioned as taking a cargo of goods in a sloop from New York to West Indies, starting Nov. 3, 1770, the consignors being merchants and others of Albany. He returned in due time, with rum, limes and cotton. Among the consignees are James Bloodgood & Co. Abraham is named among the merchants in 1794; d. Feb. 17, 1807, a. 65, James d. May 4, 1799, a 64, William d. June 29 1801, a. 41, James d. Nov. 4, 1806, a. 35, Lynot d. Enfield Ct., June 17, 1857. a. 76. S. DeWitt Bloodgood was grandson of Abraham. Of Lynot, it is said, he was born in Albany and belongs to one of those families whose names are associated with the early history and progress of our city. He was buried in Utica. We think the family came from Ct. among the earliest N. E. immigrants; were mercantile and estimable citizens.

Francis Bloodgood, b. 1768; d. March 5, 1840; gr. Yale, 1787; lawyer; one of the founders and first directors of the State Bank and for many years its president; Clerk of the Supreme Court; Mayor of the city, 1831–1833. Was also pres. of Albany Insurance Co.; distinguished for the excellence of his temper and the integrity of his character.

Lewis Boss, b. Providence, R. I., Oct. 26, 1846; gr. Dartmouth, 1870; adopting the profession of astronomer, he studied at the Naval Observatory, Washington, and was employed in government service until 1879, when he became director of the Dudley Observatory, Albany, and a professor of Astronomy in Union University. By his reported observations and published works on Astronomical subjects, he has already attained a world wide fame as a devoted astronomer of distinguished merit and promising future.

Lebbeus Booth, b. Danbury, Ct.; moved to Ballston with his father, when a boy; gr, Union, 1813; prin. Female Academy, 1815-24; md. only dau. of Ebenezer Foote, the founder; had private school at Ballston, several years; d. there Dec. 16, 1859.

John Melancthon Bradford, D. D., b. Danbury, Ct., May 12, 1781; d. March 26, 1826; gr. Brown, 1800; pastor of 1. t Reformed Dutch Church, Albany, 1802- 20; "a man of commanding presence;" "an eloquent and impressive preacher;" "among the distinguished pulpit orators of the day." His son, Alexander W., was an eminent lawyer; sometime Surrogate of New York.

John E. Bradley, b. Lee, Mass., Aug. 8, 1839; gr. Williams, 1865; Ph. D. 1879; principal of Pittsfield High School, 1865-68; and of Albany High School, from its first opening in a hall as Free Academy in 1868, with 140 pupils, to its present firm establishment, in a model building. with about 600 pupils, 20 teachers and a first-class rank among similar institutions in the country. In 1878 he visited Europe, as Commissioner at the Paris Exhibition, and made a valuable report to the State. He is known and felt in the religious, social, charitable and educational organizations of the city, and is, also, active in the interests of his Alma Mater, and of the State work for advancement of learning.

James Gordon Brooks, b. Claverack, N. Y., Sept. 3, 1801;

d. Albany Feb. 20, 1841. Son of David, a Rev. officer; gr. Union, 1829. Studied law; went to New York City, 1823; Ed. "Minerva," "Literary Gazette," "Atheneum," "Morning Courier," and cont. to "Commercial Advertiser." In 1828, md. Mary Elizabeth Aiken, of Poughkeepsie, a literary lady. In 1829, they pub., as joint authors " Rivals of Este and other Poems." In 1838 they moved to Albany.

Jonas H. Brooks, descended from one of the earliest and most respectable families of Mass.; b. Rutland, Mass., Jan. 5, 1848; studied at Oxford (N. Y.) Academy; was teacher, bank clerk and bank director, before he came to the 1st. National Exchange Bank, Albany, in 1873, as teller, and in 1881, as cashier.

Jesse Buel, b. Coventry, Ct., Jan. 4, 1778; d. Danbury, Oct. 6, 1839. A printer, he went to Albany in 1813; established and edited the *Argus* until 1821. Was a large hearted, public spirited, highly esteemed citizen. Was well known as an active and influential promoter of local institutions of religion, education and benevolence. Member of State Assembly, of the State Board of Regents, and in 1836, Whig candidate for governor of the State. He owned, occupied and successfully cultivated a large farm in the west part of the city, ever after 1821; in 1834, established the *Cultivator*, in which he, by his practical knowledge, common sense, and hearty zeal, was successful in creating a greater respect for cultivating the soil, presenting improved methods, and showing how profits could be made. He delivered numerous addresses on agricultural subjects; pub. the "Farmers Instructor" and "Farmers Companion." He lived a public benefactor, and left a great and precious name.

Aaron Burr. This man of brilliant parts, great ambition, tireless activity and questionable patriotism, studied law in Albany, having Alexander Hamilton as a fellow student; married here, opened a law office here, and was for some years well known and influential in this city. His only child, Theodosia, was born here. He was son of Aaron Burr, president of Princeton, and grandson of Jonathan Edwards, of genuine New England stock; b. Newark, N. J., Feb. 6, 1756; d. Staten Island, Sept. 14, 1836; gr. Princeton, 1772. He did service under Montgomery, Arnold, Putnam, Stirling, and Washington during four years of the Revolution ; held in N. Y. state, the offices of member of the Assembly, Att'y-General, and Com. of Claims ; was from 1791- 97, a leader in the U. S. Senate ; Vice Pres. of U. S. four years from 1801 ; killed Hamilton in a duel July 12, 1804; was tried and acquitted of treason in Aug. 1807 ; afterwards spent four or five years in London and Paris ; returned to New York in 1812, and spent the rest of his life in quiet practice of law. He was a remarkable man in his greatness and in his weakness.

Benjamin F. Butler, a descendant of Oliver Cornwell, in his maternal line ; b. Kinderhook, N. Y., Dec. 15, 1795; d. Paris, France, Nov. 8, 1858: studied law with Martin Van Buren ; became his partner in 1817 ; district atty. of Albany Co. 1821- 25 ; served in the State Assembly ; was on committee with John Duer and John C. Spencer, to revise Statutes of New York. U. S. Attorney General under Jackson, 1831- 34; acting Sec. of War, Oct. 1836 to Mar. 1837: U. S. District Atty. for Southern N. Y. 1838- 41. Joined the republican party on passage of Kansas-Nebraska bill, and voted for Fremont. After this he was instrumental in founding the University of New York, and while practising his profession, served as law professor in that institution.

Samuel Cary, b. Providence, R. I., Aug. 18, 1766; d. Bethlehem, N. Y. Feb. 16, 1845. Came to Albany, 1827; was a most acceptable preacher of the Society of Friends or Quakers; lived an eminently blameless and useful life; his influence aud example widely felt and acknowledged. His son Joseph, b. Albany Co., Jan 30, 1802; d. Albany, Aug. 29, 1879; for nearly 40 years pursued the business of a wholesale provision merchant, in Albany, in company with his brother, David H., who died in 1865. Both left unblemished and honored names.

Nathaniel Hazeltine Carter, b, Concord, N. H., Sept. 17, 1787; d. Marseilles, France, Jan. 2, 1830; gr. Dartmouth, 1811; taught in Salisbury, N. H. and Portland, Me.; read law; prof. of languages at Dartmouth, 1817- 20, In 1820 became ed. and prop. of *Albany Register*. Pub. " Letters from Europe" in 1827, after traveling there 1825- 27; spent winter of 1828 in Cuba; relinquished his paper and went to France for his health in 1829, As poems, he wrote " Burial at Sea," "Pains of Imagination," " Hymn for Christmas," and many minor ones.

Asa H. Center, b. Berkshire Co., Mass., 1779; a printer in Pittsfield; came here early in this century as foreman in the *Centinel* office; about 1805 went into mercantile business with Nathaniel Davis; dissolved and went to New York in 1827; continued business there until his death in 1857; an active, public spirited man, enjoying good will of the community.

John Chester, b. Wethersfield, Conn., Aug. 1785; d. Philadelphia, Jan. 12, 1829; gr. Yale, 1804; D. D. Union 1821; pastor of Presb. church, Hudson, N. Y. 1809- 15; first pastor

of 2nd. Presb. church, Albany, 1815- 28: amiable and sym-
pethetic as a man; fervid and persuasive in the pulpit; an
earnest worker for the education of the young and for every
worthy public enterprise; he was very useful here and endeared
himself greatly to his people. He was the pastor of DeWitt
Clinton.

Rufus W. Clarke, b. Newburyport, Mass., 1813; gr. Yale,
1838; pastor of No. Cong. church, Portsmouth, N. H., till
Dec. 1851; of Maverick church, E. Boston, 1852- 56; of So.
Cong. church, Brooklyn, 1857- 62; of 1st Reformed church,
Albany, 1862-83. D. D. Univ. of N. Y., 1862; author of
Heaven and its Scriptural Emblems; Memors of Rev. J. E.
Emerson; Lectures to Young Men; Review of Dr. Stuart on
Slavery; Romanism in America; Bible in Schools; Moody
and Sankey in England; Life Scenes of the Messiah; Heroes
of Albany; Premillennial Essays. and numerous sermons,
pamphlets and essays on various subjects. He was a faithful
pastor, a diligent workman, and did great good in this city.
He is brother of Bishop Clarke of R. I., and has four sons in
the ministry.

David H. Cochrane, of New England parentage, b. July 5,
1828; gr. Hamilton, 1850; after other teaching, was principal
Albany Normal School, 1856- 64; thence went to Brooklyn
as the president of the Collegiate and Polytechnic Institute.
To his work he has always brought scholarship, energy and
executive ability. LL D. Hamilton, 1869.

Mason F. Cogswell, b. Hartford, Conn., Nov. 10, 1809; d.
Albany. Jan. 21, 1865: son of an eminent physician and sur-
geon of same name in Conn. (1761-1830) who gr. Yale 1780.
Came to this city in 1833 and devoted himself to the duties of

his profession with almost singular zeal and fidelity. He attained a foremost rank. His own patriotic emotions and the confidence of the appointing powers are attested by his position as examining surgeon, and afterwards as hospital surgeon in important posts. He, also, heard his country's call for volunteer surgeons and readily took his place in camp and field. He was, in all places, not only the good physician, but the true man, sympathetic, genial, sincere and thoroughly upright.

John O. Cole, b. Sharon, Conn., Oct. 5, 1793; d. Albany, Jan. 4, 1878; came to this city in 1814; printer; studied law; held office of police justice forty-four years; a man of inflexible integrity, and large public respect; was always active in the interest of public morals and public education; was pres. of the Board of Education 20 years, and Supt. of Schools for eight years previous to his death. Among his sons are Addison D. and Charles W. of this city. The latter succeeds his father as Supt. of Public Instruction.

Andrew J. Colvin is a lineal descendant, through his paternal grandmother, from the Fullers of the Mayflower; an estimable citizen and lawyer. Verplanck, Supt. of the Adirondack Survey, is his son.

Charles D. Cooper, the 4th of 10 sons of Dr. Ananias Cooper; b. Rhinebeck, N. Y. 1769; ancestors among the early English Puritans of Mass.; d. Albany, Jan. 30, 1831. Came to Albany as physician in 1792; health officer, 1794-98; interested himself in politics; held offices of county clerk and county juc'ge some years; also Indian agent; was Secetary of State 1817. Noted as a man of remarkable physical force, great influence and high sense of honor. Gen. John Taylor Cooper of Albany, and Rev. Charles D. Cooper of Philadelphia, are his sons.

Erastus Corning, b. Norwich, Conn., Dec. 14, 1794; d. Albany, April 8, 1872. Went to Troy in hardware store of his uncle, Benjamin Smith, in 1807, and inherited most of his estate. In 1814, came to Albany as clerk, where he, after a few years, established the widely known and always prosperous house of Erastus Corning & Co.; was a leader for many years, in the principal business enterprises of the city, such as banks, canals and railroads; and held the most important executive offices in them. He was alderman of the city, and 3 years a Mayor; several years a member of state legislature; member of Congress 1857– 9, '61– '63, '65– '67; of the London Peace Congress, in 1861; and delegate to the State Constitutional Convention of 1867. In 1863, he retired from business with a fortune estimated at five millions, to which his son, Erastus, succeeded. He was large hearted and liberal; an unostentatious giver; a wise counselor; a public benefactor. Education, morals, charity, religion, all moved his activities. He was held in affection and honor by the friends of these causes.

Alonzo Crittenden, b. Richmond, Mass., d. Brooklyn, N. Y., 1883; gr. Union, 1824; an eminent teacher; princ. of Albany Female Acadamy 1826-45; after this, princ. of Packer Institute, Brooklyn. He was one of the pioneers in the movement favoring increased facilities for the higher education of women in our country, and practically worked with this purpose all his life.

Harry Croswell, b. W. Hartford, Conn., June 16, 1778; d. New Haven, March 13, 1858. Was a pupil of Noah Webster; D. D. Trinity, 1831. In 1802, he came to Hudson; became proprietor and editor of the *Balance*, and subsequently of the *Wasp*. Was an intense federalist and wrote vigorously and severely against his political opponents. Hamilton's last and greatest forensic effort was in his defense in a famous political libel suit. In 1808, he came to Albany and established another federal paper, an article in which led to another prosecution for libel by his opponent, Solomon Southwick, who recovered damages. Disgusted with politics Mr. C. took orders in the Episcopal Church in 1814; preached a short time at Hudson; then became rector of Trinity church, New Haven, which continued from 1815 until 1858.

Sherman Croswell, son of Rev. Harry C., b. Hudson, N. Y. 1803; d. New Haven, Conn., March 3, 1859; gr. Yale, 1822; read law; came in 1826 to Albany, and was associated with Edwin Croswell, as ed. the Argus until 1855. Was author of Croswell's Legislative Manual, which is still authority in the N. Y. legislature.

William Croswell, son of Rev. Dr. Harry, b. Hudson, N. Y. Nov. 7, 1804; d. Boston, Nov, 9, 1871; gr. Yale, 1822; studied law and pursued literary labors at Albany; then pursued theological studies at New York and Hartford, editing *Christian Watchman* at same time; rector of Christ church, Boston, 1829-40; St. Peters, Auburn N. Y., 1840-44; Church of the Advent, Boston. remainder of his life. His poems and corresponcence pub. by his father in 1833, contain some of the sweetest composition in our language. His life was a beautiful example of self-denying charity and religious devotion. D. D. Trinity, 1846.

Edwin Croswell, nephew of Rev. Dr. Harry, b. Catskill N. Y., May 29, 1797; d. Princeton, N. J., June 13, 1871. Assisted his father as ed. of the *Catskill Recorder*, supporting the War of 1812, and so managed it as to command much notice. He took control of the *Albany Argus* in 1824, changed it to a daily, and made it a leading organ of the democratic party in New York State; ranking high for the signal ability with which it was conducted, all over the country. He retired in 1854. Was State printer, 1823– 40. His literary publications are numerous, and his name and influence as a journalist will long remain.

Hooper Cumming, son of Gen. John N. Cumming, a Revolutionary officer; b. Newark, N, J.; gr. Princeton, 1805; studied theology at Andover; was pastor of the Seceders' church, as the 3rd Presb. church of Albany was then called, from 1817 to '23; resigned and went to New York city as pastor of United Presb. church; health failing, he went to Charlestown, S. C., where he died in 1825. He was a man of wonderful pulpit power, people of all classes thronging his church to overflowing every Sabbath.

Charles Davies, b. Washington, Conn., Jan. 28, 1798; ed. at West Point, 1815; LL. D. Geneva, 1840. Early worked on a farm with his father in St. Lawrence Co. Prof. at West Point, 1816– 37; at Trinity 1839– 41; New York University 1848– 49; Albany Normal School and Columbia, 1857– 65. Was paymaster in the army, 1841– 42. As a teacher of mathematics and as author of a full series of mathematical works for all grades of American Schools, he ranks unrivaled; d. Fishkill, N. Y., Sept. 17, 1876.

Amos Dean, descended from Walter, of Taunton; b. Barnard, Vt., Jan. 16, 1803; d. Albany, Jan. 26, 1868; gr. Union, 1826. Entering the profession of law, he came to Albany, and as learned in legal knowledge, always held highest rank. He was the real founder of the Albany Law School, aided by Judges Harris and Parker; from its organization in 1851, was its head professor and lecturer; also, filled the chair of lecturer on medical jurisprudence in the Albany Medical College from its opening in 1839. He projected the Young Men's Association in 1833, and was its first president. Among his many lectures and writings, the following are published:— " Medical Jurisprudence, 1854, Phrenology, 1835, Manual of Law, 1838, Philosophy of Human Life, 1839, History of Civilization, 7 Vols., since his decease. He was held in high estimation in all the stations filled by him; an eminently useful man. He was a trustee of the Albany Female Academy, Dudley Observatory, and the State Normal School; he lectured several years in the Iowa University.

Capt. Stewart Dean fitted out the sloop, Experiement, 80 tons, in Albany, and made a voyage to Canton, China, starting Dec. 1785, and returning April 1787, with a cargo of nankeens, teas, silks, and 13 sets of china ware. It was a wonder in that day and excited general interest, especially in Albany and New York. He made several voyages to China subsequently, Dean street preserves his name. He seems to have been born in Conn.; made A. his home many years, and died in New York about 1845, aged 85.

Philander Deming, of New England ancestry; b. Schoharie, N. Y., 1829; gr. Vt. University, 1861; and at Albany Law School; became stenographic reporter to the N. Y. Supreme Court, 1866; also legislative reporter; is the only Albany contributor to the *Atlantic Monthly*, and has done and is doing much literary work. He published *Adirondack Stories*.

Charles Devol; parents from Westport, Mass.; b. Schaghticoke, N. Y., April 4, 1809; gr. M. D. at Fairfield, 1831; came to Albany 1854; began to preach in 1836, as member

Troy Conference, and has since preached in Albany and many other places, and practiced medicine. He is a man of varied knowledge, a prolific essay writer, an original thinker, and a good man.

John A. Dix spent some years in Albany and made himself an interested and influential citizen. B. Boscawen, N. H., July 24, 1798; d. 1879   Did eminent military service for his country in the wars of 1812 and 1861 ; was largely useful in the Assembly and as chief executive of his adopted State of New York ; also, as its Secy. of State and Supt. of Schools ; he showed sagacious statemanship in the U. S. Senate, and wisdom in the Cabinet councils; he made a skillful diplomatist abroad ; he has written well of his travels, in his state papers and addresses. In this city his name is held in great honor as a citizen, scholar, statesman, and patriot. His good fame is national and European as well.

Lorenzo Dow preached in the early days of Methodism, here in Albany, attracting, as everywhere, crowds of listeners. B. Coventry, Conn., Oct. 16, 1777; d. Georgetown, D. C., Feb. 2, 1834.

George Dummer, b. New Haven, Conn. Feb. 8, 1782; d. Jersey City, N. J., Feb. 21, 1853; was a member of the firm of Webb & Dummer in Albany, in a wholesale store, in 1807, and did a prosperous business many years. He retired, and after a brief residence in New York, removed, in 1825, to Jersey City, where he had erected two extensive factories, one for the manufacture of flint glass, the other for making China Ware. These works did much for the growth of Jersey City. The glass factory never ceased its burning night and day for 40 years. For many years Mr. D. was leading citizen of the city, remarkable for his public spirit, common sense,

liberality, and love for order, for the useful and the good.
The laboring people always found him their true friend.

William Durant, b. Middlefield, Mass.; came to A. about
1813; d. Albany, 1845; produce merchant; trustee of Albany
Savings Bank; intelligent, energetic, successful, and liberal
in works of charity.

Clark Durant, b. Middlefield, Mass., came to A. in 1825;
bro. to William and in business with him; d. New York,
1873; very generous; gave $10,000 to the Albany Hospital;
bought and sustained the "Bethel;" gave the bell to the
3rd Presb. Church, etc. Was 1st pres. of Board of Trade;
director of Commercial Bank, etc.

William C. Durant, nephew of W. and C., came to A.,
1843; engaged in milling and flour business. William b.
Albany, gr. Princeton, late pastor of 6th Presb. church,
Albany, is a son.

Homer Eaton; b. Enosburgh, Vt., 1834; D. D. Syracuse
Univ., 1879; from 1872- 74, pastor of Grace Meth. church,
Albany, and from 1867-79, presiding Elder of Albany district.
Was in 1872 and '80, member of General Conference, and in
1881, delegate to the Ecumenical Council, London. Joel W.
Eaton is his brother.

Joel W. Eaton, b. Enosburgh, Vt., Sept. 26, 1831; gr.
Meth. Bib. Inst., 1855; D. D. Wesleyan Univ., 1881; member of Troy Conference since 1857; and came as pastor of
Ashgrove church to Albany, 1881; has been army Chaplain,
member of General Conference, and contributed largely to
the religious literature of his church.

James W. Eaton, b. New Jersey, Aug. 22, 1817; his father
a native of N. H.; came to Albany as contractor and builder

in his early manhood; in 1874 was appointed by Gov. Dix, Supt. of Construction of the State Capitol, which difficult position he held with credit to himself and advantageously to the State until 1883. Calvin W., lumber merchant, and James W., lawyer, are his sons. ,

Franklin Edson, b. Chester, Vt., April 5, 1832; came to Albany in Feb. 1852, and joined his brother Cyrus in distilling business. Here was director of State Bank, pres. Y. M. A., and vestryman of St. Paul's. In 1866, went into produce business in New York City. Has been prominent there in business circles; pres. of Produce Exchange; bank director; school trustee. Was elected Mayor of N. Y. in 1882.

Isaac Edwards, b. Corinth, N. Y., Aug. 30, 1819; d. Albany, Mar. 26, 1879; descended from good New England parentage; came to A. in 1838, and to the practice of law in 1843. With a clear, well balanced mind; accurate in knowledge; patient in hearing and weighing; fearlessly just, he became distinguished as a reference lawyer, and much employed as such, as well as in trusts and real estates. His published works on "Bailments," "Bills and Notes," "Factors and Brokers," place him among the best legal writers in the English language. For 12 years from 1867, he stood at the head of the Albany Law School; and, by his clear and thorough instructions and wise management, added much to its high standing.

Charles Lovering Elliot, of N, E. stock, b, Scipio, N. Y., Dec. 1812; d. Albany, Aug. 25, 1868. He devoted all his leisure moments while clerk in a country store to his favorite pursuits of drawing and painting. About 1834, became a pupil of Trumbull. His first attempts at portrait painting were not successful. By perseverance he came, in his later years, to rank as one of the first of American portrait painters.

Ebenezer Emmons, b. Middlefield, Mass., May 16, 1799; d. Brunswick, N. C., Oct. 1, 1863; gr. Williams; became M. D. and a successful practitioner; prof. of Natural History at Williams in 1833; made a report on Quadrupeds of Mass., and added much to the knowledge of botany, mineralogy and geology in the northern States. In 1836 was engaged upon the Geology of New York; advanced his Taconic theory in opposition to the received Silurian theory, which has since been accepted; removed to Albany in 1838, and became prof. of Chemistry in Medical college; began the geological Survey of N. C. in 1858, and was kept from returning home by the Rebellion. His reports on the Natural History of N. Y., and on the Geology and Agriculture of N. C. are very valuable, as were, also, at the time, his text books on Mineralogy and Geology.

Samuel Ware Fisher, b. Morristown, N. J., where his father was a Presb. minister, April 5, 1814; d. College Hill, Ohio, Jan. 18, 1874; gr. Yale; began preaching at W. Bloomfield, N. J.; came to Albany as pastor of fourth Presb. church, 1843; afterwards, pastor 11 years in Cincinnati, and eight years pres. of Hamilton College; finally, pastor in Utica. He was among the ablest clergymen in the church; clear, direct, affluent and vigorous in style; lofty in his themes; manly and eloquent in their utterance.

E. G. Folsom, b. Ashtabula Co., Ohio, May 1, 1821; gr. Oberlin, 1847; teacher of penmanship in public schools of Cleveland, studying, first, theology and, then, medicine meanwhile; opened Folsom's Mercantile College in 1851, in that

city; came to Albany in 1862, and has since alone and with
partners, successfully conducted Folsom's Business College
here.   He has had wide connections with several other similar colleges, and has published a valuable treatise on the
" Logic of Accounts." He is an earnest, systematic, faithful,
progressive educator.

Ebenezer Foot, founder of Albany Female Academy, b.
Conn.; a successful lawyer, practicing here in the early part
of this century; d. July 21, 1814, a. 41 years. His only
daughter md. Lebbeus Booth, second principal of the
School. Samuel A. Foot, once a prominent lawyer here and
afterwards a State Senator and county judge, was a brother.

Amos Fowler, whose father was from Lebanon, Ct., b. Co-
hocton, N. Y., July 5, 1820; gr. M. D., from Univ. of New
York, 1846; came to Albany in 1849, and has since practiced
here. Warren H. Fowler, M. D., 1879, Jefferson Med. Col.,
is a son.

William Fowler, b. East Chester, Westchester Co., N.
Y., Feb. 10, 1774: worked in manufacture of morocco in New
York City; came to Albany in 1793; lost by a great fire; was
started again chiefly by John Jacob Astor; md. Margaret Ste-
venson in 1796; was extensively engaged in wool and fur business with Benjamin Knower; retired with a good estate in
1824; one of the founders of Mechanics and Farmers Bank in
1811; a director till his death, Jan. 11, 1861. Rev. Philemon
Fowler of Utica is a son.

Samuel H. Freeman, b. Hanover, N. H., Aug. 24, 1821;
gr. Dartmouth, 1843; gr. Alb. Med. Col., 1846; for twelve
years was associated with Dr. J. H. Armsby in practice; con-
tinues practice in A.; has twice been president of the County

Medical Society, and is a member of curators of the Medical College and of the State Society.

William W. Frothingham, b. Hudson, N. Y., Sept. 21, 1796; d. Albany, Jan. 25, 1876; son of Hon. Thomas, of Charlestown, Mass., an honored revolutionary patriot who was a member of the N. Y. Senate, 1820—23, and d. at Sand Lake, N. Y., 1827 ; a successful lawyer and esteemed citizen.

Worthington Frothingham, b. Albany, Feb. 23, 1832; son of William W.; a lawyer; for 20 years United States Circuit Court Commissioner and Master in Chancery. Walter D., lawyer, is a son.

Elias Gates, b. Westmoreland, N. H., Sept. 7, 1801 ; came to A., 1825; opened a bookstore in 1830, and, until 1861, was chiefly engaged in this business at Troy and Albany, with different partners. A man of intelligence and integrity, enjoying universal respect.

Joseph E. Gavit, b. New York, Oct. 29, 1817; d. Stockbridge, Mass., Aug. 25, 1874. Settled in Albany, 1838; bank note engraver from 1841—59; carried on an extensive business in engraving in Albany; went to N. Y. City in 1859, and was instrumental in the formation of the American Bank Note Co.; became general superintendent, vice president, and from 1866, president of the Co. Devoted much of his time to the practical study of natural history and microscopy, in which he acquired extensive and critical knowledge, and remarkable skill. Was president of N. Y. Microscopical Society. His son Joseph is carrying on the work of engraving in Albany.

Horace Goodrich, gr. Union, 1814; first prin. of Albany Female Academy; d. Albany, 1815; good classical scholar;

fond of music; beloved by his patrons. He was of N. E. ancestry.

Thomas Gould, came here from R. I., and carried on the hardware business, about 1790. At first his brother, Job Gould, and Benjamin Dickinson were associated with him. After 1798, each of the Goulds carried on the same business separately; both acquired fortunes. Thomas d. April 22, 1820.

Matthew Gregory, b. Wilton, Conn., Aug. 21, 1757; d. Albany, June 4, 1848. He held commissions, and served with honor during the whole war of the revolution; came to Waterford, N. Y., 1791, and kept a small inn; and to Albany in 1803, in charge of the "Tontine," then the great hotel of the city; became proprietor of the "Eagle Tavern" in 1806; and having acquired a fortune, in 1814, bought and occupied for thirty-five years the "Congress Hall" property. He was a useful citizen, supporting all good objects; prudent in his affairs; neat, orderly, exact and prompt in all that he undertook. He was always connected, in some official position, with local matters of business, religion and benevolence.

Silvester Hale, b. Dalton, Mass., April 8, 1804; d. Albany, Aug. 27, 1881; came to Albany 1836, and carried on a large wholesale flour and grain business; served as bank director, as president of Board of Trade, and for nearly thirty years, as elder in the 4th Presb. church. His sons are William H., gr. Yale, 1860, Ph. D., 1863, a lawyer, and Lorenzo, M. D.

Matthew Hale, b. Chelsea, Vt., June 20, 1829; gr. Vt. University, 1851; 1867–8, State Senator from Essex County; settled in Albany, 1868, and is a leading member of the bar, and a prominent citizen.

James Hall, b. Hingham, Mass., Sept. 12, 1811; studied

natural sciences at the Rensselaer Polytechnic School, Troy, N. Y., 1831-36. Appointed one of the New York State geologists; he has resided in Albany since 1837, when he began to survey the western district of the state, publishing the results in 1843. Giving now special attention to paleozoic formations; he published 3 vols. on the "Paleontology of New York," in 1847-59, and is still engaged in this kind of work. He is also director of the State Museum of Natural History, the establishment, arrangement and great value of which are very largely due to his science, industry and skill. He has, also, assisted in the Canadian survey, and been State Surveyor in Wisconsin and Iowa. He has been honored by many European and American scientific societies; has contributed to their " Transactions," and written many of the government papers on fossils. His facts and opinions are known and valued wherever science is known and valued.

Jabez D. Hammond, b. New Bedford, Mass., Aug. 2, 1778; d. at Cherry Valley, N. Y., Aug. 18, 1855 ; taught school at 15; practiced medicine in Reading, Vt., when 21 ; settled in the practice of law in Cherry Valley, in 1805 ; was M. C., 1815-17; State Senator, 1817-21 ; a practicing lawyer in Albany, 1822–30; commissioner to settle N. Y. claims vs. U. States, 1825-6; visited Europe 1831; returned to Cherry Valley; was County Judge in 1838. He is author of "Political History of N. Y.," 2 vols. ; " Life and Times of Silas Wright," and "Julius Melbourne."

Ira Harris, b. Charleston, N. Y., May 31, 1802; d. Albany, Dec. 2, 1875; descended from one of the colonists who followed Roger Williams; gr. Union, 1824; came to Albany as student, under Ambrose Spencer; began his eminent legal career in 1827 ; member of Assembly, 1844-45; of State Con-

stitutional Convention, 1846-67; Judge of Supreme Court,
1847-59; U. S. Senator, 1861-67. As a legislator he was
vigilant and discreet; as jurist, impartial and learned; as a
statesman, always for country as above party. He was known,
honored, and useful in the cause of liberal learning, having
been for many years president of trustees of Union, a
trustee of Vassar, and chancellor of Rochester, beside several
similar trusts of a local character. For several years he was
· an esteemed lecturer in the Albany Law School, and president
of trustees of the Medical School. . He left a great and good
name. Hon. Hamilton Harris, of this city, late State Senator, is a brother.

Hamilton Harris, b. Preble, N. Y., May 21, 1821; of R. I.
ancestry; fitted for college at Homer and Albany; gr. Union,
1841; came to the Albany bar in 1845; practiced ever since
here; was member of Assembly in 1851; District Attorney,
1853; chairman of Republican State Committee, 1864-70;
president of Capitol Commission, 1866-75; State Senator,
1875-79. He cultivates literature; is a good writer and
speaker, an able lawyer, a shrewd politician, skilled in organ-
izing and leading. His popularity has enabled him to over-
come large opposition majorities, and succeed where others
have failed. Frederick, Union, 1875, a lawyer, is his son.

Gideon Hawley, b. Huntington, Conn., Sept. 26, 1785; d.
Albany, July 17, 1870; gr. Union, 1809; LL.D. Rutgers, 1834.
His home was in Saratoga Co. from 1794 until he was admitted
to the bar as a lawyer, in 1812, when he settled in Albany.
His tastes were for literature and science. He early and
always took a lively interest in education of the masses. He
held the office of State Supt. of Schools, 1813-18; Secretary
of the Board of Regents, 1814-41; and regent of Smithsonian

Institute, 1846–70. "Essays in Truth and Knowledge," is his only printed work outside of official papers. He was regent from 1842; and Trustee of State Normal School, Albany Academy, and Albany Female Academy, many years. "To no individual in the State are the friends of common school education more deeply indebted for the impetus given to the cause of elementary instruction in its infancy, than to Gideon Hawley." This may be, after a long and steadily useful life in many positions, his highest praise.

Henry A. Homes, b. Boston, Mass., March 10, 1812; gr. Amherst, 1830; studied theology at Andover, and medicine at Yale. From 1836–50, he was in the American Missionary work at Constantinople, followed by some three years in the American Legation, and as Charge d' Affaires at the Porte. He has been a resident of Albany since 1854, as assistant librarian or as librarian of the State Library. For his present position as chief librarian, he is eminently fitted by scholarship, cultivated tastes, and habits of research. His contributions to literature are varied in subject, and valuable to the librarian, the historian and the antiquarian. LL. D. Columbia, 1873.

Friend Humphrey, b. Simsbury, Conn., 1787; came to Albany 1811; d. March 15, 1854; leather merchant; Mayor 1843; very energetic; a very popular Mayor and most useful citizen. Gen. Chauncey Humphrey was a brother.

Isaac and George Hutton acquired wealth here in the manufacture and sale of jewelry and silver ware. They afterwards embarked in the less successful business of cotton manufacture. Isaac d. at Stuyvesant Landing, Sept. 8, 1855, aged 68; George d. at Rhinebeck. They held prominent positions in business institutions here.

Elisha Jenkins, of New England stock; his early life was spent in Hudson, N. Y.; liberally educated; pursued a mercantile life until he became wealthy; came to Albany about 1801; was State Comptroller, 1801-6, and Secretary of State three years; and Mayor of the city, 1814-19. He also filled many minor offices, and had great influence in promoting the growth of the city. He was a man of excellent sense; a gentleman in every walk of life, and carried with him into public life amenity of manners, strict integrity, and the best of business habits.

Edmund L. Judson, b. Albany, Nov. 13, 1830; s. of Ichabod L., whom he succeeded in the provision trade, 31 years ago. Was Alderman of the city, 1862-66, and Mayor, 1874-76. Nathaniel, who came here in 1796, was his grandsire, and Albert C., late County Clerk, is his brother.

James Kent, grandson of Rev. Elisha Kent, of Suffield, Conn.; b. Philippi, N. Y., July 31, 1763; spent his youth in Fairfield Co., Conn.; d. New York City, Dec. 12, 1847; gr. Yale, 1781; LL.D., Columbia, 1797. After coming to the bar, 1787, he practiced in Poughkeepsie until 1793; went to New York City; became prof. of law in Columbia; City Recorder in 1797; Judge of Supreme Court, 1798; Chief Justice, 1804; Chancellor, 1814-23. Resided in Albany during most of these last, and some subsequent years, and represented the Co. in the Const. Convention of 1821. Returning to New York City, he was prof. of law in Columbia in 1824; and in 1826-30, published his great work, " Commentaries on American Law," in 4 vols. His rank as a jurist and legal writer, and his valuable public service, are well known.

Austin H. Kibbee, of Conn. parentage; b. Malden N. Y., April 22, 1822; came to Albany in 1845; in charge of machinery of Jagger Iron Works, eight years; and has, since 1853, been in the lumber trade; has been very active in church and Sunday-school work; was Supt. Cong. Sab. School 24 years; and is now, for 13 years, pres. of directors of House of Shelter, and a promoter of other good works; also an Alderman.

George Kilbourn, b. Hartford, Conn., July 6, 1792; lived 40 years in Albany; a drum maker. James, the third of his ten children, b. Albany, March 22, 1820; died Aug. 11, 1881; carpenter by trade, and gloried in his calling; but was regarded as one of the most remarkable natural orators of the State, especially in political campaigns. He canvassed the State several times, drawing crowds, always arousing the greatest enthusiasm, by his strong logic and stirring eloquence. He sought no office; but was an honest man and a true patriot.

Rufus King, son of Charles, and grandson of the eminent statesman, Rufus; b. New York City, Jan. 26, 1814; gr. at West Point, 1833; engineer of construction at Fortress Monroe; also in N. Y. & Erie Railroad; came to Albany as writer on the *Evening Journal*; afterwards edited *Daily Advertiser*. Appointed Adj. Gen. of N. Y., by Gen. Seward; was School Commissioner for Albany Co. Removing to Milwaukee, he edited the *Sentinel*. In 1861, appointed Minister to Rome; but remained in the country, and did important service in the Union cause. In 1867 he went to Rome; d. Oct. 13, 1876.

Rufus H. King, b. Ridgefield, Conn., 1795; d. Albany, July 9, 1867. His father, Gen. Joshua King, was a distin· guished officer in the Revolutionary War. Came to Albany in 1806; clerk in retail dry goods store of Bogart & McHarg; in 1815, became one of the firm of McHarg & King; afterwards R. H. King & Co., wholesale dealers; did immense business, and acquired a colossal fortune. Taking a lively interest in

public affairs, and active in promoting worthy enterprises, he
declined political office ; but was one of the most trusted and
influential in financial circles, holding offices as director in
banks, insurance Cos., board of trade, etc. From 1840-67,
was president of State Bank. The late Col. Henry L. King,
J. Howard King, now president of State Bank, and a leading
citizen, and Gen. Rufus H. King, are his sons ; and Mrs. Gen.
Franklin Townsend, his daughter.

Benjamin Knower was from Mass., and resided in Albany
nearly 40 years. He came here a hatter, and also carried on
extensive mercantile operations. He was remarkable as a
friend to the young men in his employ, helping them, as a duty
and a pleasure, in their start in business life. His business
capacity was unsurpassed, carrying it into every worthy public
enterprise, and carrying on all his undertakings with an unsul-
lied reputation for good sense and integrity. He was one of
the founders of the Mechanics and Farmers Bank, and its
president many years. From 1821 to 1824, he was State
treasurer. As a mechanic he was confessedly· at the head ;
and by his active co-operation in founding and carrying on, for
many years, the Mechanics Institute, and the Uranian School
for the children of mechanics, did much to elevate this useful
class of citizens in his day. He died Aug. 23, 1839, a. 64.

Dyer Lathrop, b. Bozrah, Conn., May 4, 1788 ; d. Albany,
April 18, 1855 ; came to A. in 1811 ; merchant until his death.
A man of great industry, solid sense, universally respected ;
very benevolent ; was one of the founders and constant supporters of the Orphan Asylum, a leading charity of the city,
and for 24 years its treasurer.

Daniel S. Lathrop, b. Albany, April 13, 1825 ; d. 1883 ; was
his eldest son ; as a business man successful, and widely and
favorably known.

William L. Learned, b. New London, Conn., July 24, 1821; gr. Yale, with salutatory honor, 1841; ad. to bar 1844; came to Albany soon after; had Gilbert L. Wilson, James C. Cook, and Rufus G. Beardslee, as law partners; app. Justice of Supreme Court, by Gov. Hoffman, 1870, in place of Judge Peckham, deceased; elected, in fall of 1870, Judge of Supreme Court for a term of 14 years; made Pres. Justice of 3d judicial department in 1875; professor in Albany Law School now for several years; president of trustees of Albany Female Academy; LL.D., Yale, 1878. John De Witt Peltz, lawyer, married a daughter.

Noah Levings, b. Cheshire Co., N. H., Sept. 29, 1796; d. Cincinnati, Jan. 9, 1849; D. D. Union; came to Troy, N. Y., as a blacksmith, when 16; began to preach at 21; ministered in very many towns and cities; at Albany, 1840. One of the leaders of the Methodist church in this vicinity in his time.

Robert Lewis kept the most popular tavern in his day, cor. of what is now So. Pearl and State St.; d. June 17, 1798; succeeded by his son, Stewart. It was the resort of the leading citizens, and of all distinguished visitors of that day.

John Lovett, b. Conn.; gr. Yale, 1782; attempted a school in Albany soon after; read law; resided as tutor and land agent at Ft. Miller; then at Lansingburgh; member of Assembly, 1800-1-7; returned to A. in 1812; was on the staff of Gen. Van Rensselaer; member of 13th Congress; afterwards went to Ohio; was interested in the first steamboat on Lake Erie; d. Ft. Meigs, Ohio, Aug., 1818.

Addison Low, b. Shrewsbury, Vt., Nov. 21, 1809; d. Albany, Aug. 1, 1883. Came here in 1822; father carried on furnace and machinery business. In 1865 he was appointed, by Prest. Johnson, local inspector of steamboats; subsequently supervising inspector of steamers in the waters from Cape May to Portland, Me., including Philadelphia, New York and Boston. He aided in the construction of the present laws in regard to steamboats. Resigned in 1879, and afterwards acted as consulting mechanical engineer and designer of engines. W. G. Low and W. H. Low are his brothers, and William, the artist, is a son. His daughter Mary is wife of Judge Danaher.

Jonathan Lyman, b. Derby, Conn., June 7, 1786; d. Schodack Landing, N. Y., Dec. 5, 1856; came to A. 1815; architect and builder; superintended building old City Hall, old State House, and Female Academy; was a man of sterling qualities of mind and heart. His son, Charles R. Lyman, b. Albany, 1818; assistant city surveyor; flour merchant; Mary Augusta, teacher in Female Academy, is a granddaughter.

Henry Strong McCall, b. Lebanon, Conn., Feb. 14, 1819; gr. Yale, 1842. Came to Albany as principal of Boys' Collegiate Institute, located on Broadway, and taught and read law until 1847, when he was admitted to the bar. He has ever since resided and practiced law in this city; was county Superintendent of Schools in 1847, and has been actively identified with the advancement of the public schools of this city. Was city Attorney from 1854 to 1856. He was active in founding the Congregational Church in 1850, and has always been the clerk and held other offices in it. In 1851, he published "Notes to the N. Y. Civil Procedure," which has had 3 editions; in 1860 "the Clerks' Assistant," which has reached 3 editions; in 1862 "the Constable's Guide," of which 3 editions have been issued; in 1865, the "New York Civil and Criminal Justice," of which the 5th edition has been published; and in 1883, a work of 400 pp, on "Real Property." "His writings are used by a larger number of lawyers than those of any author engaged in the active duties of the profession." He has been, since 1879, a lecturer in the Albany Law school. As an upright, sound, clear headed lawyer, he has no superior. Henry S. McCall, Jr., lawyer, is a son.

Stuart McKissick, b. Saco, Me., Nov. 27, 1807; d. Albany, Aug. 29, 1882; came to this State in 1816; a long time engaged in the transportation and commission business in Onondaga Co., and in Troy and Albany; later, dealer in flour and produce; held important business trusts here in banking and mercantile organizations, and as member of the school board, and of the Presbyterian Church.

Elisha Mack, b. Middlefield, Mass., Sept. 26, 1784; d. Albany, Nov. 24, 1854; general merchandise; a very worthy man. Elisha Mack, son of Elisha, b. Windsor, Mass., Feb. 7, 1811; came to A. 1816; clerk for his father; police officer from 1838, about 30 years, when Loveridge, Kane and Cole were police justices; and was always regarded as a remarkably skillful detective of crime, and a most reliable man in any position in which he was placed. Many very dark and important cases were brought to light by him, in the interest of justice and public order.

Elisha L. Magoon, b. Lebanon, N. H., Oct. 20, 1810; early a brick layer; ord. Baptist preacher 1840; preached as pastor in Richmond, Va., Cincinnati, New York and Philadelphia; settled in Albany as pastor 1st Baptist ch. 1857. His ministry is one of power; his public influence decided for every good work. Has published "Orators of American Revolution," and several other works bearing on eloquence, religion and patriotism.

Alden March, b. Sutton, Mass., Sept., 1795; d. Albany, June 17, 1869; .gr. Brown Med. School, 1820; began practice in Albany, 1820; in 1821 began a private school of medicine and surgery, which he continued until the Albany Med. Coll. was founded, in 1839. Of this, and of the Albany Hospital, he was one of the founders, and the recognized head as long as he lived. He was a quick and skillful surgeon, and made many important improvements. He devoted himself to his profession, and was regarded as unsurpassed in surgery in this country. As an example of his zeal, he selected and took from Boston in a wagon, his anatomical illustrations for his private school. At this time there were only one hospital and two medical schools in the State. The admirable system of college clinics is due to him. As a citizen, he had all the elements of a public-spirited, Christian manhood. Henry, M.D., Albany, is his son.

Five brothers, born in Lyme, Conn.,— Uriah, John, William, Alexander and Richard Marvin,— came here about the year 1800; and three of them carried on in partnership, with some changes, the grocery business for more than 40 years, with great success. They were William, who retired in 1828, and d. New London, Conn., May 19, 1849 aged 74; John, who retired 1822, and d. Albany, May 8, 1853; and Alexander, who retired in 1842, and d. Albany, Sept. 1, 1864, in his 80th year.

Thomas Mather came from Lyme, Conn., and opened a store early in the present century; later had a mill on Wynants-kill, and dealt in flour and grain; and finally carried on business with the West Indies, from Middletown, Conn., where he died at an advanced age, about 1850. He was one of the first directors of the New York State Bank. Elias and Samuel, also merchants in Albany, were his brothers, and the present enterprising and successful mercantile firm members of of Mather Bros. are grandsons.

Arthur D. Mayo, b. Warwick, Mass., Jan. 31, 1823; studied at Amherst, and with Dr. H. Ballou; preached in Gloucester, Mass., Cleveland and Cincinnati, O., and Springfield, Mass. In 1855, came to Albany, as pastor of Unitarian Society. He is a fine writer, and has published several interesting addresses and other writings. His educational papers are pointed and valuable.

William L. Marcy, b. Southbridge, Mass., Dec. 12, 1786; d. Ballston, N. Y., July 4, 1857: gr. Brown, 1808; taught school; studied law; practiced in Troy; distinguished himself in the war of 1812; Adj. Gen. 1821; State Comptroller 1823; Judge of Supreme Court 1829; U. S. Senator 1831; Governor of New York 1833-9; U. S. Secy. of War 1815-49; U. S. Secy. of State 1853-7. He resided in Albany many years, as a public officer and valued citizen. He was a scholar, a statesman, a writer, and a diplomatist of remarkable ability. Simple in his habits, a hard worker and faithful man, eminently useful to his country and his kind. His grave is in the Rural Cemetery.

Nathaniel C. Moak descended from the Clevelands of Woburn, Mass.; b. Schoharie Co., Oct. 3, 1833; studied law; admitted to practice, 1856; has practiced in Cherry Valley and Oneonta; came to A. in 1867; Dist. Atty. 1872; has been engaged in many important criminal trials; is a great worker and student; has a library valued at $50,000; is much engaged in editing law works; has already published some thirty volumes.

Joel Munsell, b. Northfield, Mass., April 14, 1808; d. Albany, Jan. 15, 1880. Came to Albany as a printer, in 1827. He was a remarkably busy man; a first-class printer; a patient and judicious compiler and editor, with exceeding fondness for American history and antiquities. For the preservation, by the printer's art, of local and documentary history, all American historians will always be indebted to him. He published and edited the *New York State Mechanic, The Unionist, Albany State Register, Statesman,* and *Morning Express;* also, Albany Annals, 10 vols.; Historical Collections, 4 vols.; " History of Printing; " " Paper and Paper Making; " " Historical Papers," 10 vols.; and numerous smaller works. His invaluable aid by counsel, annotations and type work has contributed greatly to the literary merit and mechanical beauty of many works in genealogy, antiquities, biography and history bearing his imprint. For many years he was a leading spirit in the Albany Institute.

Eliphalet Nott, b. Ashford, Conn., June 25, 1773; d. Schenectady, N. Y., Jan. 29, 1866; gr. Brown, 1795; D.D. Princeton, 1805; began to preach in 1795; preached and taught at Cherry Valley, N. Y.; was first native New England pastor in Albany, being pastor of 1st Presb. church from 1798-1804. As a preacher he was regarded as very eloquent, attracting large congregations. As a citizen, interested in every good work, he commanded profound respect and great influence. From 1804 until his decease, he was the popular president of Union College, leaving a deep and abiding impress on hundreds of young men. In this position his usefulness to Albany was inestimable, because very many of its " boys " were placed under his instruction. He was a practical man, as shown in his improvements in stoves, the benefits of which all buildings warmed by them still enjoy. Many of his writings are published; but his great life work was written in the imperishable minds of young men.

Thomas W. Olcott, son of Josiah, of Stratford, Conn.; b. Hudson, N. Y., May 22, 1795; d. Albany, Mar. 23, 1880. Came to A. as clerk in the Mechanics' and Farmers' Bank, at its opening, July 29, 1811, and continued, as cashier, from July, 1817; as president from June, 1836. During his long career as banker, for nearly 70 years, with singular devotion, he attained a reputation as bank financier second to no one in the country; and left large wealth, and a name greatly honored for benevolent deeds, broad public spirit, and exalted integrity. In 1863 he declined a flattering offer from Pres. Lincoln, of the position of the first Comptroller of the Currency. He declined all public office, except such as related to the promotion of education, or other local interests. He leaves one daughter and five sons, Dudley and John J. now president and vice president of the M. and F. Bank; Frederic P. late State Comptroller; and Alexander and Theodore, of Corning, N. Y.

David Perkins Page, b. Epping, N. H., July 4, 1810; d. Albany, N. Y., Jan. 1, 1848; attended Hampton Academy a short time; began to teach district schools; at 21 was principal of English department of Newburyport High School, where he spent 12 years of severe study and faithful, discriminating labor, and gained a reputation that made him first principal of Albany Normal School. His labors for nearly 4 years assured the "experiment" a success, and gave the institution a lease of life which it still holds in vigor; and gave himself a name among American teachers that cannot die. The "Elementary Chart of Vocal Sounds," and "Theory and Practice of Teaching," are his printed works. He was buried in the cemetery at Newburyport.

Erastus D. Palmer, of New England descent; b. Pompey, N. Y., April 2, 1817. A carpenter until 29; a cameo-cutter until 35 : he came to Albany and became a sculptor. He has never studied abroad, but has produced over 100 works in marble, which have secured a foremost rank among American sculptors. Among them are "Infant Ceres," "The Sleeping Peri," "The Little Peasant," "The White Captive," "Resignation," "Spring," "The Infant Flora," and "The Angel at the Sepulchre;" together with bas reliefs, and "Landing of the Pilgrims;" and 15 statues intended for the Capitol at Washington.

Ray Palmer, b. Little Compton, R. I., 1808; gr. Yale, 1830. D.D., Union, 1852; pastor in Bath, Me., 1835–50; and first pastor of the Congregational Church, Albany, 1850-65. His work here was laying foundations, and he laid them well. He has since been Secy. of Am. Cong. Union, New York. He has written many lyric hymns and other verse, some of which will always be sung in the churches. He has also published many sermons, addresses, religious books and memoirs.

William Parmelee, b. Lansingburgh, N. Y., 1807; d. Albany. Mar. 15, 1856; gr. Yale, 1826; practiced law in Albany from 1830; City Attorney 1836; County Judge 1839, and 1847-52: City Recorder 1840-46; Mayor 1846 and 1855. He died while yet holding this office. He married Helen, daughter of Dr. T. Romeyn Beck.

John Davis Parsons, b. East Hampton, L. I., April 27, 1815; of Puritan ancestry; came to Albany early in life, and as the managing member of the printing, binding and publishing house of Weed, Parsons & Co., is widely and favorably known. Much of the State printing and best law printing is done by this house.

L. Sprague Parsons, b. Walcott, Conn., May 16, 1809; gr. Yale, 1837; principal of Albany Female Academy, 1845-55; had previously taught 6 years in a select school here; d. Cohoes, N. Y., Apr. 27, 1864.

Rufus W. Peckham, of Rhode Island ancestry; b. Rensselaerville, N. Y., Dec. 20, 1809; drowned on the sea-wrecked steamer, Ville du Havre, Nov. 22, 1873; gr. Union, 1827; district attorney for Albany Co.. 1838-41; Judge of Supreme Court 1859, and re-elected in 1867 without opposition; elected Associate Judge of Court of Appeals for a term of 14 years, 1870; 1852-54, member of Congress. With a clear head, strong assertion of honest convictions, and commanding presence, he was powerful as an advocate; with learning, and keen sense of justice added, he made an eminent judge; and was, withal, too independent and patriotic to be a partisan. Wheeler H., of New York, and Rufus W., of Albany, recently elected to the Supreme Court Bench, are his sons.

Eli Perry, of Connecticut ancestry; b. Johnstown, N. Y. 1802; d. Albany, May 17, 1881. Mayor of Albany 6 years; M. C. 2 years; very influential in civil affairs and financial circles, and did much good with his wealth.

John S. Perry, b. Dec. 17, 1815, in Farmington, Ct.; came to Albany in 1830, as clerk in crockery store of H. & C. Webb & Co.; in 1843 went into the manufacture of stoves and machinery; 10 years later confined his business to improving, making and selling stoves, which, with different partners, he has continued ever since, with remarkable success. Since

1864 his partners have been his cousin, Nathan B. Perry, and Andrew Dickey, from Wilton, N. H. Their annual product of stoves has gone up, in 40 years, from 500 tons to 12,000 tons, now exceeding any other foundry in the world. Mr. P. was the first to introduce the base burner, which has culminated in the argand burner, which has revolutionized the coal-heating stoves of this country. He was for 3 years pres. of the U. S. National Asso. of Stove Manufacturers, which he helped organize   He is prominent in the financial and religious organizations of the city.

Amasa J. Parker, son of Rev. Daniel; b. Sharon, Conn., June 2, 1807; gr. Union, 1825; LL.D. Geneva, 1845; prin. Hudson Academy at 16; ad. to bar in 1828; practiced at Delhi until 1844, when he came to Albany; member of Assembly 1834; regent 1835; M. C. 1836–40; Circuit judge and Vice Chancellor, 1844–47; Judge of Supreme Court, 1847–55; of Court of Appeals, 1854; many years lecturer in Albany Law School, of which, with Dean and Harris, he was a founder. Memb. State Const. Conv., 1867; twice dem. candidate for Governor. Has largely interested himself in education; trustee of, Cornell, of Albany Med. Coll., and Female Academy. Of fine culture, broad views, independent conviction, and careful and accurate legal knowledge, he is widely known and highly esteemed for his learning, wisdom and integrity. Col. Amasa J., lawyer, is his son.

George R. Perkins, born of New England stock, Otsego Co., N. Y., May 3, 1812. LL. D. Hamilton, 1852; taught at Clinton Institute, 1831–38; at Utica Academy, 1838–44; in Albany Normal School, 1844–52, of which he was principal 4 years. Superintended the building of Dudley Observatory, and was, in 1858, asst. eng. and surv. of the State. He was author of a text book on astronomy, and of a series of mathematical text books; a large contributor to educational journals; d. Aug. 22, 1876.

Amos Pilsbury, son of the best prison warden of his time, Moses C. Pilsbury, of the N. H. and Conn. State Prisons, was born Londonderry, N. H., Feb. 8, 1805; d. Albany, July, 1873. Was deputy under his father at Concord, N. H., and Wethersfield, Conn. After his long and successful service at Albany Co. Penitentiary. he resigned his position and went to London, in 1872, under appointment from Gov. Hoffman, as Commissioner to the International Penitentiary Congress, and made an able report to the State on his return. Few men have lived more useful lives, or left a more honored name.

Louis D. Pilsbury, son of Amos, was born at Wethersfield, Conn., and as Superintendent fully sustained the high name of the Penitentiary, which his father had given it. He has held until recently, the position of State Superintendent of Prisons.

Ananias Platt. kept Tontine Coffee House three years, closing with May, 1801 ; had kept a public house in Lansingburg, and was a pioneer stage proprietor of line from Albany to that town ; d. April 10, 1842, a. 80.

Charles H. Porter descended from one of the oldest and most respectable of N. E. families ; is a scholarly gentleman, a leading physician in Albany; and for some years, one of the faculty of the Medical College.

Horatio Potter, of N. E. ancestry; b. La Grange, N. Y., Feb. 9, 1802: bro. of Bishop Alonzo; gr. Union, 1826; D. D. Trinity; LL.D. Geneva; D. C. L. Oxford; Rector of

St. Peter's, Albany, 1833–54, where he was eminently honored and useful; cons. provis. bishop of New York in 1854, and became bishop of the diocese in 1861. Is father of the late Hon. Clarkson Potter, and of Eliphalet Nott Potter, president of Union College. Bishop P. md. the only dau. of Prest. Nott.

Daniel J. Pratt descended from William, of Saybrook, Ct.; b. Westmoreland, N. Y., Mar. 8, 1827; gr. Hamilton, 1851; principal of Fredonia Academy, 1854-64; Assistant Secretary of Board of Regents since 1866; Secretary of Albany Institute since 1869. Besides the most assiduous and intelligent devotion to his official duties, he has done a great amount of collateral faithful work. as author or editor of valuable reports, essays, and other contributions to the educational and historical literature of the State. The suggestion, systematizing, and practical working of the Board of Regents, are largely due to his patient industry.

Harmon Pumpelly, b. Salisbury, Conn., Aug. 1, 1795; d. Albany, Sept., 28, 1882. After spending his earlier life in Tioga Co., as land surveyor and agent for large land holders, and laying foundations for fortune himself, he came to Albany, in 1841, where his business forethought, promptness and integrity were in requisition until his death. He had been, for many years, president of the Albany Savings Bank, Albany Insurance Co., and Albany Gas Light Co., and filled other important trusts in the city, especially in St. Peter's church. Mrs. James Kidd, and Mrs. John Meredith Read, are his daughters.

Elisha Putnam, nephew of Gen. Israel; b. Dutton, Mass.; md. daughter of Capt. Stephen W. Johnson, of the " Boston Tea Party." Came to A. about 1790; architect and builder;

put up first nail machine in this vicinity; first to propose carrying water in iron pipes; patented hooped stave raceway for mills; Supt. of City Water Works about 1800; built St Peter's, North Dutch, and old 1st Presb. churches; engineer, about 1820, on Erie Canal; long an elder in the Presb. church. After 70 years old, wrote and published "Crisis; or the last trumpet;" d. Feb. 11. 1854, a. 89.

Jared L. Rathbone, b. Salem, Conn.; d. Albany; carried on a stove foundry; was an Alderman, and also Mayor of the city, 1839-40.

John F. Rathbone, b. Albany, Oct. 9, 1819. After some time as student and clerk, he went into the foundry business, in 1840; built a stove foundry in 1845, and is now at the head of one of the largest in the world, under firm name of Rathbone, Sard & Co. In 1861-7, he was Brig. Gen. of 9th Brigade of National Guards, and commander of forces sent into the military service in the civil war; 35 regiments were sent forward by him. He founded the Rathbone Library of the University of Rochester.

Matthew H. Read, b. New Haven, Conn., Sept. 2, 1803; d. Albany, Sept. 6, 1883; came to this city about 1830; engaged in the flour and grain trade, retiring in 1860. Was prominent in commercial circles; president of First National Bank since 1869; leaves four sons and three daughters.

Marcus T. Reynolds, of Connecticut ancestry; d. Albany, July 11, 1865; a distinguished lawyer; represented the city in the State Legislature; was actively interested in the Albany Hospital, Orphan Asylum, and other humane institutions; also in the railroad enterprises that centered in the city; was a highly useful and respected citizen. Dexter Reynolds, lawyer, is a son, and Marcus T. and Leonard Hun, lawyers, are grandsons.

Charles A. Robertson, son of Conn. and Mass. parents; b. Mobile, Ala.; gr. Harvard, 1850; studied medicine at Boston and Philadelphia; settled in Albany, and rapidly rose in his profession, making the eye and ear a specialty. Was talented, public-spirited, and of restless energy; wrote much, and to the point; prest. of Y. M. A., and member of school board; d. 1879.

Ebenezer Platt Rogers, b. Dec. 18, 1817; d. Montclair, N. J., Oct. 22, 1881; educated at Yale and Princeton. Interrupted much by weak eyes, and poor health. Was pastor at Chicopee and Northampton, Mass., Augusta, Ga., Philadelphia and New York city. Came to Albany as pastor of 1st Reformed church, in Nov. 1856, and spent 6 years of " useful, acceptable service, " especially endearing himself by his ready personal sympathy. D. D., Oglethorpe, 1853. Published many sermons and other religious writings.

Joseph Russell, b. Bedford, Mass., Oct. 7, 1777; came to this city in early manhood; became an active and prosperous merchant in the firm of Thomas and Joseph Russell; always influential in commercial circles; an honorable man; d. Dec. 25, 1838. Joseph W. Russell, Esq., a lawyer of this city, is a grandson.

Luther Sawyer, b. Lancaster, Mass.; came to A. 1813; brick and stone mason. His son William Sawyer, b. March 14, 1821; shoe dealer; " never drank, smoked or chewed;" never attended a circus or theatre; is now in real estate speculations; has large income, with which he is doing much good, especially in helping Baptist churches and the poor.

John G. Saxe, b. Highgate. Vt., June 2, 1816; gr. Middlebury, 1839; practiced law in Vt., 1843- 50; ed. *Burlington*

Sentinel, 1850- 55; 1851, State Atty. for Vt.; candidate for Governor. Has resided for many years in Albany. His poems, chiefly of wit and humor, are widely read and some of them have become a part of our nation's permanent literature. They have been published at different times and in various editions.

Theodore Sedgwick, son of Judge Theodore Sedgwick, b. Sheffield, Mass., Dec. 31, 1780; d. Pittsfield, Mass., Nov. 7, 1839; gr. Yale, 1798; practiced law with great distinction, in Albany from 1801- 22; was the first to suggest the idea of a railroad from Albany to Boston over the Green Mountains, and carried it through in the Mass. legislature, of which he was a member in 1824. '25. '27. Devoted friend of free trade, temperance and anti-slavery, and published writings on these subjects. *Theodore,* his son b. Albany, Jan. 27, 1811: d. Stockbridge, Mass., Dec. 8, 1859; gr. Columbia, 1829; practiced law in New York city; U. S. Atty. for So. District of New York; author of Life of Wm. Livingston, Writings of Wm. Leggett, and many treatises on political economy and law

John and Robert F. Slack, brothers; b. Weston, Mass: came to A. about 1810; enterprising and successful wholesale grocers for more than 30 years; also largely engaged in lumber and stave business; word as good as their bond; warmly interested in education and every good work. Dr. Henry of Fiskill, and Mrs. George B. Steele of A., are surviving children.

Elihu Smith, b. Stamford, Conn., Mar. 14, 1804; came to Albany, 1847; architect and builder; had previously lived in Genoa, Ithaca and Troy; began making stove models in 1830; claims invention of the principle of base burning and argand stoves; also of improved refrigerators; is a skillful mechanic and an honest man.

Horace E. Smith, b. Weston, Vt., 1817; LL. D. Dartmouth, 1880; practiced law in Boston in New York city and in Johnstown, N. Y.; in 1879 became Dean of Albany Law School. He has been a prominent member of the Mass. legislature and of the Constitutional Convention of New York, 1867; and has had extensive practice in his profession. He is a man of high purposes, diligent work, eminent legal knowledge, and excellent qualities for his present position.

Norman L. Snow, son of Hon. Dr. Simon Snow of Mansfield, Mass., b. Root, N. Y. Apr. 7, 1839; gr. Union, 1859; N. Y. College of Phys. and Surgeons, 1861; rendered important service as army Surgeon during the late civil war; began a successful practice in Canajoharie when the war was over and held honorable civil positions in that village; visited the hospitals of Europe in 1873; settled in practice in Albany with Dr. A. Van Derveer in 1875; and is holding high rank in the Medical College, in the Hospital, in the Medical Society, and in general practice.

Solomon Southwick, b. Newport, R. I., Dec. 25, 1773; d. Albany, Nov. 18, 1839. Came to this city, 1792; became connected with the *Albany Register*, published by Robert Barber, whose sister he married; and succeeded him as proprietor in 1808. It was the leading paper of his party, and he the leader until 1817. He held the offices of State printer, Clerk of the Assembly, Sheriff of the County, president of the Mechanics' and Farmers' Bank, postmaster and regent of the University. Twice he was the candidate for Governor; when 40 years of age, he was admitted as attorney at law. Besides the *Register*, he conducted the "*Ploughboy*," "*National Observer*," "*Christian Visitant*" and "*Family Newspaper*." He lectured extensively on temperance, education and morality, and published valuable treatises on these and kindred subjects. He was a remarkable man; with strong convictions, great boldness, untiring devotion, and great ambition. During his later years, he devoted all his high powers to doing good.

Ambrose Spencer, b. Salisbury, Conn., Dec. 13, 1765; d. Lyons, N. Y., Nov. 13, 1848; gr. Harvard, 1783; LL. D., Harvard, 1821. About 1785, he entered upon the practice of law in Hudson, N. Y., and was called, almost at once, to important office in that city, and in the State legislature. In 1802-4, he was Atty. General and began to reside in Albany, which was his home until 1839. He became Justice of the Supreme Court in 1804, and Chief Justice from 1819-23; member of N. Y. Const. Conv. in 1821; M. C. 1829-31. In this city he held many important offices, including that of Mayor. He was truly a great and good man, one of the shining lights of his time. His legal decisions stand as highest authority. In political counsels he had great weight. At the same time, like all truly great men, he was simple hearted, approachable by all who needed sympathy and counsel, and as just and inflexible as Cato.

John C. Spencer, son of Ambrose; b. Hudson, N. Y., Jan. 8, 1788; d. Albany, May 18, 1855; gr. Union, 1806; practiced law in Canandaigua; settled in Albany, 1845; was nearly his whole life in public business; besides minor offices, M. C., 1817-19; State Assembly, 1819-20; State Senate, 1825-28; 1832, Assembly; 1839-41, Sec. of State and Supt. Com. Schools; 1841, Sec. of War; 1843, Sec. of Treasury. Had much to do with looking into the affairs of the old U. S. bank, and also with the anti-masonic excitement. The organization of the State Asylum for Idiots, and the improvement of the

State common school system, are largely due to him. The most useful part of his life was spent in this city. His annotated " De Tocqueville's Democracy in America," and his great labor in revision of the Statutes of the State, are among his monuments.

William B. Sprague, b. Andover, Conn., Oct. 16, 1795; d. Flushing, L. I., May 7, 1876; gr. Yale, 1815; Princeton Theo. Sem., 1819; D. D. Columbia, 1828; settled at W. Springfield, Mass., 1819-29; pastor of 2d Presb. church, Albany, 1829-70. Such a long ministry is unusual in a city, and it was filled by him with distinguished honor. His heart was warm toward all good, and he was very helpful in good works. He had a facile pen and his published works are very numerous; among them are over 100 pamphlets, many religious books, memoirs, and notes of travel. His great work, "Annals of American Pulpit," in 9 vols., is a monument of industry amid other labors. His autograph collection was the largest in America.

John and Spencer Stafford were prosperous merchants, in company here for many years, from about the beginning of this century. The former died Oct. 12, 1819, aged 57; the latter, Feb. 10, L844, aged 72.

Horace C. Stanton, b. Wolfborough, N. H.; gr. Union, 1867, at head of his class; excels as a linguist; read law; then went to Princeton Theol. Sem., and gr. 1873; pastor 3 years in Edinburg, N. Y.; came to Albany as pastor of Clinton Sq. Presb. Church, 1876. B. I. Stanton, lawyer, is a brother.

Eben S. Stearns, b. Mass.; gr. Harvard, 1841; had been prin. of a Mass. Normal School; prin. Albany Female Academy, 1855-66; afterwards prin. Robinson Female Seminary, Exeter, N. H.

Lynot Bloodgood, merchant.
William Bloodgood, merchant.
John Boardman.
Edward Brown, merchant.
Samuel Brown, merchant.
Aaron Burr, lawyer.
Richard Cartwright.
Isaac W. Clark, editor.
Walter Clark, merchant.
Elisha Crane, merchant.
Stewart Deane, shipper.
Samuel Dexter, druggist.
Thomas S. Diamond, d. 1796, a. 59.
Benjamin Dickinson, merchant.
Elisha Dorr, hatter.
Christopher Dunn, taverner.
James Elliott, city marshal.
John Ely, teacher.
Thomas W. Ford, merchant.
William Fowler, merchant.
Joseph Fry, printer.
Elihu Goodrich, teacher.
Job Gould, merchant.
Thomas Gould, merchant.
Matthew Gregory, taverner.
Daniel Hale, lawyer.
Daniel Hale, merchant.
Hamlet H. Hickcock.
Isaac Hodge, d. 1806., a. 84.
Philip Hooker, builder.
Elias Hosford, bookbinder and publisher.

Elijah Hosford, bookbinder and publisher.
John Hudson, stage proprietor.
Chauncey Humphrey, merchant.
George Hutton, silversmith.
Isaac Hutton, silversmith.
Thaddeus Joy, shipper.
Nathaniel Judson, merchant.
Enoch Leonard, physician.
Robert Lewis, taverner.
Stewart Lewis, taverner.
John Lovett, lawyer.
Alexander Marvin, merchant.
John Marvin, merchant.
Richard Marvin, merchant.
Uriah Marvin, merchant.
William Marvin, merchant.
Elias Mather, merchant.
Samuel Mather, merchant.
Thomas Mather, merchant.
William Newton.
Eliphalet Nott, clergyman.
Isaac Packard, mechanic.
Aaron Pennell.
Obadiah Penniman, bookseller,
Ananias Platt, taverner and stage proprietor
Abram Powers, baker.
Ralph Pratt, merchant.
John Price, d. 1781, a. 68.
Elisha Putnam, builder.
Thomas Russell, merchant.
Joseph Russell, merchant.

John Stearns, b. Wilbraham, Mass., May 16, 1770; d. New York, Mar. 18, 1848; gr. Yale. 1789; went to Waterford, N. Y., 1793; to Albany, 1810; to New York City, 1819. Was in 1806, founder of the State Medical Society, of which he was the first secretary, and four years president; also first president of the New York Academy of Medicine, in 1846; member of N. Y. Senate, 1809–13. A leading aim of his life was to purify and elevate the profession of medicine. To this and his own personal culture, he devoted his vigorous mind, his untiring energy. His influence was very great.

Lemuel Steele, b. Hartford, Conn., Aug. 26, 1787; d. Albany, Dec. 26, 1853; came to A. 1815; engaged in manufacturing and importing paper-hangings until 1852, when he was succeeded by his son, George B. Steele, and Robert M. King; now succeeded by Frank B. King. Mr. S. was a prominent citizen, holding various offices; was 10 years an Alderman; 20 years or more a bank director; and several years Chief Engineer of the Fire Department.

Moses W. Stickney, b. Antrim, N. H.; d. Albany, Feb. 4, 1879; came to A. in 1836. Leander Stickney, bro. of M. W.; b. Antrim; d. 1882; came to A. in 1838. Both were Coffee and Spice Manufacturers and merchants, of the firm of Bacon, Stickney & Co.; successful in business, and acquired large wealth.

Alfred B. Street, descended from Rev. Nicholas Street, of New Haven; b. Poughkeepsie, N. Y., Dec. 18, 1811; d. Albany, June, 1881; studied and practiced law with his father, at Monticello, N. Y.; came to Albany, 1839; Librarian of State Library for some years. An unostentatious, but highly esteemed citizen, he has left a name honored by his literary work. Besides numerous contributions to periodicals, and

poems on anniversary occasions, he has written, " Burning of
Schenectady," "Frontenac," "History of the Council of
Revision," " Woods and Waters," " Forest Pictures," " Indian Pass." Some of his poems have been collected, and
published in volumes.

Jonathan Tenney, b. Corinth, Vt., Sept. 14, 1817; gr.
Dartmouth, 1843; studied law and medicine, but never prac-
ticed; has also been a licensed Congregational minister.
Early chose teaching as a profession; has been a successful
principal of academies and high schools in N. H., Mass., and
N. Y., about 25 years; was founder and president of the N. H.
Teachers' Association, in 1854; has been Commissioner of
Schools, member of State Board of Education, and secretary
of the same, in N. H.; Deputy Supt. of Public Instruction in
N. Y.; has lectured extensively on educational subjects, and
conducted teachers' institutes in Vt., N. H., Mass., Me., R. I.,
and N. Y.; has written much for educational and literary
periodicals, as editor and contributor; was Supt. of Schools
in Owego, N. Y., and Chairman of School Board in Manches-
ter, N. H. His historical, statistical, biographical and educational publications, have been numerous. He came to A. in
1868; has been 7 years Librarian of Y. M. A., and is now
engaged in literary work for publication. Received honorary
degree of Ph.D. from Dartmouth, in 1880.

George H. Thacher, descended from Rev. Thomas Thacher,
first pastor of the Old South Church, Boston, was born in
Hornellsville, June 4, 1818. He is grandson of Judge Hor-
nell, for whom this town was named. About 1848, he came
to A., and went into the stove foundry business with Billings
P. Learned, which he left in 1852, to establish the manufacture of car-wheels, which for 30 years has been successfully

John Shepherd, d. 1797, a. 48.

Elisha W. Skinner, printer and publisher.

Solomon Southwick, printer and editor.

Thomas Spencer, printer.

Joab Stafford, merchant.

John Stafford, merchant.

Spencer Stafford, merchant.

George W. Thacher.

William Thompson, d. 1797, a. 32.

Isaiah Townsend, iron manufacturer.

John Townsend, iron manufacturer.

Israel Tuffs.

Oliver Warner, d. 1796, a. 21.

Elkanah Watson, merchant.

John M. Watson, d. 1795.

Charles R. Webster, printer and publisher.

George Webster, printer.

John W. Wendell, hatter.

William Woods, d. 1799, a. 66.

While it will be admitted that we owe much here in Albany and all over our land, to the love of civil and religious liberty, the firm principles, the pure faith, and the hardy, resolute, persevering enterprise of our Puritan ancestry, no one ought to abate one iota from the credit due the hospitable, frank, independent, stout-hearted, cautious Netherlander of the Hudson Valley, nor from the true-hearted, faithful, enduring, bright, liberty-loving Huguenot, who early cast his lot among our fathers. From all these together, did this country derive the elements of its wonderful greatness and power, its broad and ever expanding institutions.

We would be glad if harmony with our purpose in this

essay allowed us to speak more fully of the talents and vir-
tues, of the patriotism, liberality, and honor that shone forth,
all along the early history of struggle and growth in our
Hudson river valley, even down to later times, connected with
the names of Van Rensselaer, Schuyler, Gansevoort, Ten
Broeck,· De Witt, Lansing, Wendell, Yates, Van Schaick,
Van Vechten, Van Buren, Van Loon, Bleecker, and other
Holland families; nor would we forget the English Clintons
of illustrious fame, nor the Scotch Livingstons, nor the
Huguenot Jay, nor the Irish Montgomery, nor the German
Herkimer, nor the Prussian Steuben, nor the Polish Pulaski,
nor the French Lafayette, all of whom did great service in
doing noble deeds to protect this valley when it most needed
them, and left a record of shining worth.

Among the movements of a minor and local character
that indicated a new element in the city after 1780, we find,
mostly from the papers of the period, the following:

In 1771, a printing office was started and the *Albany
Gazette* issued,—first newspaper, so far as known, in the city.
Discontinued during the Revolution.

1779, Capt. Machin engaged in taking a water level between
Albany and Schenectady, with aim of supplying the city with
water by means of aqueduct.

1782. CHARLES R. WEBSTER, associated with S. Balentine,
started the *New York Gazetteer*. It discontinued in 1784.

1784. A *Pocket Almanack*, first work of the kind issued in
the city, was published.

CHARLES R. WEBSTER, May 28, issued the first uumber of
a new paper called the *Albany Gazette*, which continued
until its 72d year, 1845.

Several stores offering a variety of goods, including drugs, hats, nails, and East India and European goods, "for cash or barter," were advertised this year, indicating a new activity in business. Among these traders were JOHN W. WENDELL, "a Bostonian," manufacturer and dealer in hats. We detect several other New England names among these "merchants" and "artisans," such as Maj. Daniel Hale, Capt. Abraham Bloodgood, J. Hutton, "minister of the gospel," and Robert Lewis, keeper of the leading tavern for many years.

1784, July 4. The day was celebrated with "thirteen guns" in the morning, and illumination of the city in the evening.

Select schools and dancing schools were advertised as opening in the summer and autumn.

Nov. 8. *Webster's Calendar and Albany Almanack*, appeared for 1785. It was No. 1,—but it has been annually issued ever since, Munsell continuing it after the death of Charles R. Webster.

1785. A mail from New York City twice a week. *Gazette* enlarged.—A law for killing all dogs was passed.—Theatrical exhibitions appeared, approved by a "a large and respectable part of the community." CAPT. STEWART DEAN fitted out the sloop Experiment, and sailed from this port for China. It returned safely, April 22, 1787.

1786, July 22. The corporation and citizens celebrated the centennial anniversary of the charter of the city. The number of houses at this time was 550. Boston had four times as many.

1788, Aug. 8. The ratification of the adoption of the United States Constitution by the State of New York, on the 26th of July, was celebrated by an imposing procession, a public dinner, toasts, speeches, firing of guns, and a street fight between the federalists and the anti-federalists.

1789. The *Gazette* was published twice a week.

1791. The city was engaged in paving streets.—A hand-fire engine was purchased.—A market-house was built.—A subscription for a library was raised. It is said to have been started as early as 1785 by a subscription of 100 members at $5 each share, and 10 per cent. annual payment.

1792. A project was set on foot to establish a College in Albany by gift of land for a building by the corporation, and subscriptions from citizens. It resulted in establishing Union College at Schenectady. A meeting was held to discuss the project of a bank. It was incorporated as the Bank of Albany, April 10, 1792, the first in the city and the second in the State. It continued until May 11, 1861. Daniel Hale and Elkanah Watson were among the first directors. Efforts were making to connect Hudson River with Lake Ontario by means of canals and rivers. Elkanah Watson was an active leader in the enterprise. The street paving business was kept up amid much excitement as to width and expense. A better supply of water was agitated. A scheme for building a new and large hotel was discussed at a public meeting. It was kept up for some years and resulted in the erection of the Tontine, which was first kept by Ananias Platt, and afterward by Matthew Gregory. Most of the hotels in Albany for many years were kept by men from New England ; and stages were run and mails carried by them.

1793. Stages had been, for some time, run to Bennington. It was now proposed to run them to Whitestown, connecting with post carriers on to Niagara. C. R. Webster had associated with him his brother GEORGE WEBSTER, and they were receiving and forwarding letters with their paper, to every part of the country where there were no mails. This was the enterprise of true New Englanders. On Jan. 10, one hundred and fifty mechanics held a meeting and organized the *Albany Mechanic Society*, which was noted for its activity and usefulness It continued many years, and largely promoted the intelligence, zeal. skill, and public respect of its members. Among its first officers were JOHN W. WENDELL, President; CHARLES R. WEBSTER, Vice-President; ISAAC HUTTON, Treasurer. The manufacture of maple sugar was encouraged, a new thing in this section. ELISHA DORR appears as a hat manufacturer and dealer in cider. Every one seemed full of business, and business of many kinds novel in this city, was tried.

In May, a law passed by the common council went into effect, ordaining that no gutter or spout should project from any building into the street: that the water should be conducted down the sides of the houses within three feet of the ground by pipes, under a penalty of 40£. This was done by the " new comers " who had succeeded in getting a majority in the city council, and was an innovation against a custom brought from Holland and honored by long years. Its enforcement caused much feeling among the old inhabitants. Webster, Seymour and Ensign, started the first paper mill in this quarter. The building was erected in Troy. Stage lines were extending. One to Ballston ; another to Canajoharie, another to Northampton. EZRA AMES, appears as painter of portraits, signs, carriages. standards, etc. The lighting of the streets begins to be discussed. The most destructive fire that has occurred in the city in all its history took place Nov. 17 ; estimated loss $250.000. The good President Dwight, who visited the city subsequently, and saw the new buildings and other improvements, regarded it as a special blessing.. The city council established a night watch.

1794. Trade in wheat and other agricultural products was greatly increasing. Vigorous efforts were making to connect Seneca Lake with Albany by canals. The citizens subscribed £6000 towards locating a college in this city. A large portion of this amount was subscribed by men who had immigrated from New England. Influences were made to bear upon the Regents to locate it in Schenectady. Paving the city was nearly completed, and made Albany " from one of the filthiest to one of the cleanest cities in America."

1795. Albany County received £1500, being its portion of the school money of the State, under its first appropriation of £20,000. Glass works had been carried on for some time successfully; Elkanah Watson. and Thomas and Samuel Mather, and two others, constituted the manufacturing company. A water passage was opened between Albany and Oswego. by canals and rivers. Great delight was expressed at the lighting of the city.

1796. JOHN CLARK and REUBEN KING run a mail stage, occupying 4 days through between Boston and Albany. The numbering of the houses was talked of. A new Presbyterian church was erected. Mail facilities were rapidly increasing. JOSEPH FRY printed a paper called the *Chronicle*. Albany became the capital of the State.

1797. Philip Hooker. Christopher Batterman, and Elias Putnam, were the leading architects and builders of the day. Much is said of the improvement in dwellings and hotels. The " two steeple " Dutch church was building.

1798. Eliphalet Nott, the first native New England preacher, was installed pastor of the Presbyterian church, Oct. 3. The day of building turnpikes was dawning. The first Catholic church was built, the city giving the ground, and citizens aiding by subscriptions.

1799. Sabbath breaking by pleasure riding and keeping open places of traffic, was forbidden by city ordinance as against good morals. Improvements by removing obstructions to navigating the Hudson were making. A circulating library was opened by Solomon Southwick and associate.

These are given as examples of the new activity that had been stirring the city for the last ten or fifteen years before 1800. We have no room to pursue this method further. It will be seen that great changes, for that day and in such a city as it had been, were taking place. A writer at the beginning of this century speaks of certain natives of New England as being "among all the popular movements of the day." Another remarks that "all enterprises had a live Yankee in them."

As illustrations of the state of feeling towards the early movers in the reforms introduced into Albany by the Eastern immigrants at the close of the last century and the beginning of this, we give the following anecdotes connected with the doings of Elkanah Watson, one of the foremost of the reformers. That relic of an old European usage, the purchase of the freedom of the city, obtained in this city at the time of his coming, in 1789. It was necessary to secure a new settler in the enjoyment and protection of his rights of citizenship. Mr. Watson, on the 28th of May, 1790, paid £5 to Mayor Lansing for this certificate of freedom. He knew the power of the press, and often used it without stint. This abuse was vigorously attacked by him and soon abolished.

At the time of his arrival, as he states, there were not more than five New England families resident in the city. The streets were ungraded, unpaved, and unlighted. It made matters worse that the eave spouts projected over the streets,

as they did over the canals in Holland, and often poured their
contents on the heads of the traveler who was obliged to be
out in the rain.   The streets were very miry, and vehicles
were often stuck so fast in them as to get on with difficulty.
Added to all this, they were frequented by swine that rooted
in the mud and garbage in them.   Many of the best citizens
regarded these animals very useful as public scavengers.   The
keen and restless mind of Mr. Watson, with his eastern ideas,
and the culture that his residence in European cities had given
him, could not fail to notice these things and urge through
the press and by personal effort, radical improvements.   He
generally succeeded in accomplishing his objects, but not
without entailing expense and other inconvenience.   The
hostility against his schemes and his person were, at one time,
very strong.   Time, which often reveals lasting real good
coming out of present seeming ill, brought him gratitude and
praise.

Nothing, if we can believe an observer of that day, could
exceed the consternation of the old burghers when they
learned of the order of the city council to cut off these
spouts.   "Had it been a decree abolishing their mother
tongue, it could hardly have excited greater astonishment, or
greater indignation.   They rallied their forces and secured
the election of Mr. Watson, to the heretofore useless office of
"hog constable," as an expression of their disgust toward him.
The next morning found him in the streets driving the street
scavengers to the public pound.

Mr. Watson uses his own words.   " Just after State street
had been paved at a heavy expense, I sauntered into it
immediately succeeding a heavy thunder storm, and whilst
regretting the disturbance in the sidewalk, and to observe

the cellars filled with water, * * * I heard two women, in the act of clearing their invaded premises from the accumulation of mud and water, cry out, —" Here comes that infernal paving Yankee." "Then they approached me in a menacing attitude, broomsticks erect. Prudence dictated a retreat to avoid being broomsticked by the infuriated Amazons. * * I walked off at a quick pace."

Hoping that we have clearly shown the state of society and the progress of events down to the beginning of this century, we proceed to present some of the leading institutions that have, if we may credit the records and the memory of man, been suggested, projected, or progressed chiefly by New England men and motive, with the names of some of those who have been most prominent in them ; to be followed by some general statements in regard to certain classes of business and professions, and closed by such biographical sketches as we have been able to procure, chiefly of the departed ones. We suppose it is well to regard the sentiment,—Pronounce no man happy until he is dead.

It may be understood that every person named in these connections, is of New England birth or ancestry.

ALBANY ACADEMY. Some of the first movements toward establishing an Academy for boys were made while Rev. Dr. Nott was pastor in the city, he being one the chief movers. These were continued by such men as John M. Bradford, Theodore Sedgwick, Ambrose Spencer, Chauncey Humphrey, James Kent, Ebenezer Baldwin, Gideon Hawley, James Goold, Thomas W. Olcott, Charles R. Webster, Theodoric R. Beck, from New England, and kindred spirits among the Holland descendants, until it was established, by the aid of the city council and citizen subscriptions, in 1813, and put in full operation in 1815. For thirty-one years, Dr. Beck, gave it the impress of his great character. Among the principals who have followed him have been George H. Cook, James W. Mason, Abel Wood, and notably for twelve years, ending in 1882, Merrill Edward Gates, now president of Rutgers' College, all of New England ancestry and character. It has always held a high rank among the many excellent schools of its kind in our country. Hundreds of the boys of Albany have received their literary discipline and their best inspirations to act well their part, in this noble institution.

ALBANY FEMALE ACADEMY. A "Union School" for the higher education of Albany girls was started in 1814, by Ebenezer Foote, a lawyer from Connecticut. It was supported by tuition. Out of it grew, in course, the present flourishing "Girls' Academy," incorporated under the above title in 1821. Its first trustees show the names of James Kent, John Chester, Gideon Hawley, Asa H. Center, Joseph Russell, William Fowler. Since then, there has always been a preponderance of New England men on the board of trustees, — among them William L. Marcy, Wm. B. Sprague, Ira Harris, Edwin Croswell, Marcus T. Reynolds, Thomas Gould, Isaac Hutton, Dr. John Stearns, Nathaniel Davis, John Q. Wilson, Harmon Pumpelly, Ezra P. Prentice, James H. Armsby, Amasa J. Parker, William L. Learned, Rufus W. Clarke, and Erastus D. Palmer.

The architect of its model building was Jonathan Lyman. Alonzo Crittenden, of Massachusetts, 19 years; Eben S. Stearns, of New Hampshire, 12 years; L. Sprague Parsons, of Connecticut, 10 years; have been the principals whose labors have given it a wide extended and good fame; while, for shorter terms, in its early years, it was taught by Horace

Goodrich, Lebbeus Booth, and Fred'k Matthews, from New England. Its present able principal, Miss Lucy A. Plympton, is from Massachusetts, and is successfully sustaining its character.

PUBLIC FREE SCHOOLS. There were no school facilities for the education of the children of the people of Albany worthy of mention before the establishment of the above Academies. This fact is spoken of with regret in the newspapers of that day. Private schools, usually ephemeral, and taught by indifferent teachers, were patronized by the wealthy. The citizens generally were given to trade and material improvements, so that little organized effort was made to secure first class public schools, much less free schools for all. In 1810, there were no public schools. A school called the Uranian Academy, projected and sustained for the benefit of the children of mechanics, by such New England mechanics as Charles R. Webster, Thomas Russell, Isaac Hutton, Elisha Dorr, Benjamin Knower, and others, had then existed for several years, and continued awhile after 1820. The Lancasterian System, inaugurating a school managed on a popular plan at cheap rates of tuition, was favored by Gideon Hawley. A school of that class was started here about 1812, and continued about twenty-five years. It was well patronized and very useful. But it was not a free school.

The public school system of the State was of slow growth. Something of the kind, in ideal, had many admirers, many advocates. The New England idea was early brought here but modifications and improvements that led to much talk and much writing with little practical result, were brought forward by governors and school officers from 1812 down to

1868, when the really free public school system of the State
was first presented to the people of the State of New York,
through the earnest and persistent efforts of Victor M. Rice,
a man of New England blood, ideas, and energy. But before
this, much had been accomplished by Gideon Hawley, Jede-
diah Peck, Jabez D. Hammond, John C. Spencer, John A.
Dix, Daniel D. Barnard, James Wadsworth, Francis Dwight,
Calvin T. Hulburd, Alonzo Potter, John A. King, Samuel
Young, William L. Marcy, and other New England men of
great influence. Their efforts were for the whole State.
Until the State system was settled, there could be said to be
but little real system in Albany. The more prospered classes
of the city seemed satisfied with the advantages offered by
the truly excellent academies, and some very good private
schools. For some thirty years before 1868, Albany had
public schools ; but the odious rate bills were a burden for
the poor, and there was general indifference among the rich.
For the excellence of our present system, growing better
every year in its practical working, much is due to such men
as John O. Cole, George W. Carpenter, John G. Treadwell,
James L. Babcock, Henry S. McCall, and others, supported
by a liberal public sentiment, which has been promoted by
the good work of John W. Bulkley, Thomas W. Valentine,
of the past, and Josiah H. Gilbert, Levi Cass, John E. Sher-
wood, John A. Howe, Eli E. Packer, and other principals of
the grammar schools, with the able faculty of the high
school of to-day, named elsewhere.

ALBANY STATE NORMAL SCHOOL was opened May 7, 1844,
as an experiment, being the first in the State. In 1848, it was
made permanent. A building was erected, and opened for
pupils, July 31, 1849. Ever since then, it has had an able

corps of teachers, a large patronage, and enjoys the fullest confidence of the State and of all friends of education. Its inception was by New England minds, among them Samuel Young, Alonzo Potter, Gideon Hawley, and Francis Dwight. Its principals, Page, Perkins, Cochrane, Woolworth, Alden, and Waterbury, have been of New England stock, as has been a large number of its assistants and pupils, both male and female. It is soon to be removed to a new site on Washington Park, having a building unsurpassed for architectural beauty and working adaptation.

DUDLEY OBSERVATORY was named in honor of Hon. Charles E. Dudley, a native of England, who came to Newport, R. I., while a boy, received his early culture and pursued his vocation of merchant there, and came to Albany in 1811. He married Blandina Bleecker in 1809; held an influential, social, and civil position in Albany; was State Senator, 1820-'25; Mayor, 1821-28; U. S. Senator, 1829-33. d. Albany, Jan. 23. 1841. After his decease, Mrs. Dudley contributed $105,000, which, with liberal contributions from Thomas W. Olcott, and other citizens, made the amount $200,000, and founded the institution, with land, buildings, and instruments. Incorporated 1852; dedicated 1856. Dr. James H. Armsby is acknowledged to have been the most active citizen in working up the interest which secured the necessary funds. At the dedication, Ira Harris presided, and Washington Hunt, Edward Everett, and Louis Agassiz made the addresses. Prof. Benjamin A. Gould, of Boston, was the first astronomer in charge. The present Director of the Observatory is that already widely known and very talented son of Rhode Island and graduate of Dartmouth, Prof. Lewis Boss. Since he came here, about eight years

ago, the institution has been rapidly advancing in reputation
among scientific astronomers abroad as well as at home. At
present, about two thirds of the trustees are men of New
England origin.

ALBANY INSTITUTE grew out of the " Society for Promotion of Useful Arts," started in 1791, and the "Albany·
Lyceum of Natural History," of early date. It was chartered
in 1829; embraces most of the men of literary and scientific
tastes in the city; holds regular meetings for papers and dis-
cussions; has a library of 6,000 volumes, besides pamphlets
and papers; and has published 10 volumes of transactions and
proceedings. Dr. T. R. Beck was its founder, upbuilder, and
president for many years. Other New England men have
done their full share in its literary and financial support.
Among them may be named. Joel Munsell, Daniel J. Pratt,
James Hall, James H. Armsby, Amos Dean, Henry A. Homes,
Charles M. Jenkins, and many others.

ALBANY MEDICAL COLLEGE grew out of a class in medicine
and surgery started in 1821, by that most eminent surgeon,
Dr. Alden March. He was afterwards joined by his· brother-
in-law, almost equally eminent in his profession, and quite
equal in important public enterprises, Dr. James H. Armsby.
These two are its acknowledged founders. Its first course of
lectures began in 1839. It now constitutes a part of Union
University. Its library, largely selected by Dr. T. R. Beck,
is valuable; its museum is unequalled in this country and
unsurpassed in Europe; its chemical and anatomical facilities
are all that can be desired; its standard is very high. It numbers a faculty of about 20; has had about 5,000 students, and
1,500 graduates. Besides its founders, it has numbered in
its learned faculty, very many of the most eminent medical
lecturers from New England.

ALBANY LAW SCHOOL. Organized 1851; now a branch of Union University; to Amos Dean is chiefly due its organization; has graduated about 2,000 students. Its principal lecturers in the faculty have been Amos Dean, Horace E. Smith, and Matthew Hale from Vermont; Amasa J. Parker, William L. Learned, and Henry S. McCall from Connecticut; Ira Harris, from Rhode Island; Isaac Edwards, from Massachusetts; all men eminent in legal lore, and residents of the city. Amasa J. Parker and Ira Harris should be named with Amos Dean as the founders of the institution. It now has a separate building and is rapidly growing in patronage

DANA NATURAL HISTORY SOCIETY. This is an institution named in honor of Prof. James D. Dana, of Yale College; organized in 1868; its active members, ladies of scientific tastes and culture; holding stated meetings for papers and discussion; pursuing studies in classes; having frequent field meetings, often joined by Albany Institute. Among its presidents have been Mrs. William Barnes, (daughter of Thurlow Weed) 1 year; Mrs. Dr. Daniel J. Pratt, (b. Mass.) 1 year; Mrs. Dr. John E. Bradley, (of High School) 2 years; Mrs. Dr. Jonathan Tenney, (b. N. H.) 6 years; and Mrs. R. D. Williams, 1 year. It is a useful and growing institution, reflecting great credit on its originators and managers.

ST. AGNES SCHOOL, a very admirably planned and conducted school for girls; was founded by Rt. Rev. William C. Doane, Bishop of Albany, in 1870; incorporated in 1871; school opened in 1872. The wealth of the large hearted, liberal minded Erastus Corning, Sen., secured the grounds for the fine buildings; and further aid, united with the energetic work of Bishop Doane, erected and furnished them and the cathedral close by. The promise of a prosperous future is very bright.

YOUNG MEN'S ASSOCIATION. Amos Dean was one of its founders and first president. It was the outcome of a demand of the young men of 1833, in which year it was founded, for an organization for mutual inprovement in public speaking and better facilities for periodical and library reading. It has done a great deal of good; the only institution in the city that contains a reading room and library, so cheap as to be almost free; accessible to every citizen. It is not large, but has much of what is most called for in Albany. Erastus Corning, Sen has been its most liberal benefactor. Among others have been Thurlow Weed, Thomas W. Olcott, Joel Munsell, and Angelo Ames. Of its presidents. besides the first, Charles A. Hopkins, John Davis, Denison Worthington, Walter R. Bush, Arthur C. Southwick, Rufus King, Charles H. Stanton, Franklin Townsend, William A. Rice, George B. Steele, James I. Johnson, Theodore Townsend, George C. Lee, Ralph P. Lathrop, Charles T. Shepard, Edmund L. Judson, Franklin Edson, Frank Chamberlain, Grenville Tremain, Henry C Littlefield, Charles A. Robertson, Amasa J. Parker, Jr. Frederick W. Brown, Thurlow W. Barnes, John M. Bigelow, William P. Rudd, Frederick Harris, and Oren E. Wilson, are of New England antecedents.

ALBANY ORPHAN ASYLUM. This city was formerly reproached for its lack of institutions of charity and benevolence. Now they have become very numerous, varied in their special objects, and well sustained.

It was said by the traveler Buckingham in 1838, " Albany is singularly lacking in benevolent institutions compared with the other older cities of America, or with the extent of its own population, wealth, and resources." He visited the orphan asylum and gave quite an extended account of what he saw, with decided approval.

Among the first established and one of the best managed,
is this asylum for orphans. It was opened in 1829, largely
through the activity of native New Englanders. Its principal
supporters have been James D. Wasson, John F. Rathbone,
Ira Harris, John O. Wilson, Eli Perry, James Dexter, Dyer
Lathrop, Isaac Edwards, James Covert, Justus F. Taylor,
Jeremiah Waterman, William G. Thomas, James D. Wasson,
Marcus T. Reynolds.

ALBANY HOSPITAL owes its existence to Dr. James H.
Armsby, whose untiring efforts made with heartfelt and
intelligent zeal and much sacrifice, gave it plan, secured it
means and successful operation. No institution in the city
has now a more popular interest. It was incorporated in
1849. In its list of governors are to be found many of our
best citizens; and the very best physicians and surgeons
have from the beginning given their attendance.

THE ALBANY HOMEOPATHIC HOSPITAL. Organized in
1868, and is supported and managed chiefly by such men as
Erastus Corning, Amos P. Palmer, Nathan B. Perry, and
M. V. B. Bull.

THE CHILD'S HOSPITAL, recently established, constitutes
a part of the Christian work done by the Cathedral of All
Saints, under the direction of the Episcopal Bishop, Rt. Rev.
William C. Doane, and supported by Erastus Corning and
others.

HOME OF THE FRIENDLESS, a retreat for aged women, was
established in 1850, by Mrs. Lee, and a suitable building
erected subsequently on a lot given by James Kidd. Its
management is by ladies, many of whom, it may be observed,
are of New England ancestry.

HOUSE OF SHELTER. Organized in 1868, a home for once

fallen, now repentant women, owes its existence and great usefulness chiefly to the labors and benefactions of Austin S. Kibbee.

HOME FOR AGED MEN. Originated by James B. Jermain in 1876. He has given to it freely of his time and ample means. It receives the encouragement and support of the best men and women of the city.

WASHINGTON PARK. This most attractive and popular institution of Albany, is the legitimate outgrowth and expression of the progressive spirit introduced into the city by the New England immigration. It lies west of the capitol about one mile, and on an elevation about two hundred feet higher than the Hudson. Its establishment was long opposed as creating a large and needless expense. But, at length, in 1869, a commission was constituted by state law, and it became a fact. It has since been increasing in acres, in improvement, and in public favor. Most of the ground occupied, once a graveyard. a pasture, and a military muster ground, is now a charming landscape, with hill and dale and lake, with drives, walks and resting places; tastefully laid out and cultivated. It is surrounded more and more every year, by handsome residences occupied by some of the best citizens of the city. Reuben H. Bingham was the first surveyor, and John Bridgford one of the first commission. It contains over one hundred acres.

ALBANY COUNTY PENITENTIARY, was erected in 1845-46 While specially a county prison, it receives convicts from all parts of the country, particularly from the United States courts, and from other State counties, on payment of board Amos Pilsbury was its superintendent from 1846 to 1872, except five years spent in charge of the reformatory on

Ward's Island, and as Superintendent of the Metropolitan
Police, New York City. The silent system, so called, was
adopted at the start, and has ever since been successfully kept
up. Convicts are treated kindly but firmly; — eating and
sleeping in their cells; marched to and from them to their
work, in lock step; never speaking to each other; always
kept employed. The institution has secured a wide reputation for discipline and financial profit. LEWIS D. PILS-
BURY succeeded his father from 1872-79. The managment of
the Pilsburys, by universal consent, has given this penitentiary its wonderful success and universal admiration, beyond
any other in the Union, be it state, county, or city. It has
furnished example to the best institutions of the kind more
recently established   It has often had as many as one thou·
sand convicts at one time.

ALBANY RURAL CEMETERY. This oft frequented city of
the dead, last earthly home, " life's fitful fever o'er," of many
who have lived here, sprang from a powerful sermon preached
by Rev. Dr. Bartholomew T. Welch, in December, 1840. It
was repeated by request; followed by a public meeting, Dec.
31st; an act of incorporation in 1841; purchase, laying out,
and working; and a consecration in 1844. The first board
of trustees contains the names of Rev. Dr. B. T. Welch,
John A. Dix, J. Q. Wilson, A. M. Strong, T. W. Olcott, E.
P. Prentice, E. Baker, and Ira Harris. Others since have
been Erastus Corning, Dudley Olcott, John F. Rathbone, E.
D. Palmer, J. B. Jermain, R. W. Peckham, W. L. Marcy, and
others.

At the consecration, Daniel D. Barnard was the orator:
Alfred B. Street the poet; Revs. Dr. W. B. Sprague and H.
Potter, were the clergy; and active on that day and in the

whole work, as long as they lived, besides the trustees, were
Gideon Hawley, Amos Dean, Otis Allen, Lewis Benedict,
Matthew Patten, and many others. Gen. Rufus King was the
marshal. In natural and artistic beauty, this cemetery has
been spoken of by good critics as excelled only by that at
Cincinnati. Its location is about three miles north of the
city.

CHURCHES AND CLERGY.

DUTCH REFORMED. This ancient church has been largely
helped in its growth in this city by those able ministers of
New England antecedents, John M. Bradford; 1805-20;
Ebenezer P. Rogers, 1856-62; Rufus W. Clarke, 1858-83;
John Ludlow, 1823-33; Thomas E. Vermilye, 1835-39;
Dwight K. Bartlett, 1873-81. Many of its leading lay-mem-
bers, also, were New Englanders.

LUTHERAN. While this church, the second established in
the city, never had a pastor from New England, several of
its leading members have been and still are New Englanders.
Joel Munsell attended here.

EPISCOPAL. Ministers of this church first came here,
probably, as chaplains to the English garrison at Fort Frederick, after it came in possession of the English in 1664.
English missionaries were sent here at the beginning of the
18th century. The first church, located about where St. Peter's
now is, was opened in 1716. For many years New England
has contributed many of its most active and influential
members to this church. And it has given, at least, among
its clergy, Horatio Potter, Timothy C. Pitkin, Wm. C. Doane;
probably several others.

PRESBYTERIAN. A church seems to have been organized by a few Scotch and English resident Presbyterians in 1763, soon after the close of the French war. It was closed during the Revolution, and re-organized the latter part of 1785. Then entered it most of the New England immigrants. They seem to have been prominent. Among the trustees, deacons, and elders, we find the following New England names:— John W. Wendell, Boston, James Bloodgood, Joseph New-land, John Folsom, Isaac Hutton, Charles R. Webster, Enoch Leonard, Francis Bloodgood, George Pearson, William P. Beers, Dr. Elias Willard, John Boardman, Ananias Platt, Chester Bulkley, Thomas Mather, Eleazer F. Backus, John Marvin, Elisha Dorr, Willard Walker, Isiah Townsend, William Fowler, James King, Rufus H. King, Levi Philips, Cr. Alden March, Abraham Covert, Amos Fassett, Elihu Russell, with others from southern counties, from New Jersey, England, and Scotland. Eliphalet Nott was its pastor from 1798-1804.

In 1813, was organized the 2nd church, which was more decided still in its New England membership, so much so that Elias Putnam, the architect, with reference to this fact, placed on the spire what he called a pumpkin and a codfish, as appropriate emblems. John Chester, (1817-26), and William B. Sprague, (1829-70) were the honored pastors for a period of fifty out of seventy years of its existence.

New England has also, I think, given to the Presbyterian churches of this city, Hooper Cumming, Henry R. Weed, Ezra A. Huntington, Edward D. Allen, Samuel W. Fisher, William H. Williams, Benjamin N. Martin, A. H. Dean, Samuel T. Seelye, Henry Darling, William Durant, and Horace C. Stanton, most of them eminent for learning, piety, and eloquence, widely known and greatly useful. This city

has been greatly favored and the good in it promoted by
the pastors of the Presbyterian churches.

METHODIST. Methodism was first, we think, brought here
from New England, and has been built up and established in
a most prospeious condition, mostly by preachers of New
England origin. It is said that a church was formed here as
early as about 1790. Now there are six Methodist churches.
Among the preachers have been Samuel Merwin, Tobias
Spencer, Lorenzo Dow, Elijah Hedding, Noah Levings,
Charles Sherman, Alfred Saxe, John Lindsey, Charles Devol,
Jesse T. Peck, Samuel McKean, Homer Eaton, J. E. C.
Sawyer, D. W. Gates, Joel W. Eaton, and doubtless several
others, who have been most efficient church builders and
christian workers.

BAPTIST. The first church was organized in 1810; there
are now five flourishing churches of this denomination in the
city, containing a large number of prominent and active
members of New England birth or descent. Among their
ministers have been, Elias L. Magoon, Bartholomew T.
Welch, Francis R. Morse, and Henry M. King, all men of
potent influence, some of them of great power. We think
that several other Baptist pastors came from New England
families.

CHRISTIAN. The earnest and vigorous pastor of this
church, is Edgar C. Abbott, of the extensive and respectable
New England family of that name. This church is now
taking a new departure of growth and influence under his
labors.

ROMAN CATHOLIC. When a house of worship in this city
for this church was first called for, in the latter part of the
last century, the men of New England, with wonderful liber-

ality, contributed of their money and their influence, and secured its erection. REV. CLARENCE A. WALWORTH, gr. Union 1838, son of the late chancellor, Reuben H. Walworth, rector of St. Mary's. He is a man devoted to temperance and other works of christian benevolence, and highly esteemed in the city.

QUAKER. This quiet and exemplary sect began to hold meetings here about 1825, and organized and built a meeting house in 1835. Among its leading laymen and preachers it numbers Samuel Carey, of Rhode Island, and others from New England.

UNITARIAN. Though not strongly organized here, this denomination is composed of an intelligent class, mostly from New England, and has had the preaching since about 1840, of such able divines as Orville Dewey, Henry F. Harrington, A. D. Mayo, George T. Simmons, and Charles G. Ames.

CONGREGATIONAL. This strong church is the direct outgrowth of the New England sentiment of this city. It was founded in 1850, by men coming out peaceably, from honest conviction of duty, mostly from the Presbyterian and Reformed churches of the city. Among them were such New England men as Anthony Gould, James Gould. Bradford R. Wood, Rufus H. King, Henry S. McCall, Uriah G. Bigelow, Theodore D. Smith, John G. Treadwell, Chauncey P. Williams, Isaac Edwards, William L. Learned, and many others. Ray Palmer, (1850-66) was its first pastor,—succeeded by William S. Smart, since 1867. It has the reputation of holding in its congregation, more of the liberally educated men of the city than any other church.

COLLEGES. Union, so near to Albany, has given college

training to most of its young men. Princeton, Rutgers,
Columbia, and Hamilton, have taken many of them through
their liberal culture. But New England has had its full share
of influence in this kind of preparation for life work. The
following, after much research, shows, as nearly as we now
can ascertain, the number of men who have graduated from
New England colleges and have spent more or less of their
active lives in Albany, viz:—Bowdoin, 1 ; Waterville, 1 ;
Dartmouth, 12 ; Middlebury, 4 ; Vt. University, 3 ; Harvard,
21 ; Amherst, 12 ; Williams, 41 ; Brown, 9 ; Trinity, 4 ;
Middletown, 7 ; Yale, 63.   Here are potent influences.

Since institutions of New England became well established
here, the city has chosen many natives of New England or
their descendants, as chief executives in the office of mayor.
We believe the following belong to this class :—

1814-19. Elisha Jenkins.

1821-24. Charles E. Dudley.

1828-31. Ambrose Spencer.

1832-33. Isaiah Townsend.

1831-32. }
1833-34. } Francis Bloodgood.

1834-37. Erastus Corning.

1838-41. Jared L. Rathbone.

1843-45. }
1849 50. } Friend Humphrey.

1845-46. John Keys Paige.

1846-48. }
1853-56. } William Parmalee.

1850-51. Franklin Townsend.

1851-53. }
1856-60 } Eli Perry.
1862-66. }

1860-62. }
1866-68. } Geo. H. Thatcher.
1870-74. }

1874-76. Edmund L. Judson.

The influence of all these men upon the advancement of the city, cannot be too highly estimated.

The New York Governors have all had a temporary home in Albany; and some have resided here many years, and taken an active part in its local affairs. Among them the following are of New England ancestry.

1833-39. William L. Marcy.
1839-43. William H. Seward.
1845-47. Silas Wright.
1847-49. John Young.
1849-51. Hamilton Fish.
1851-53. Washington Hunt
1853-55. } Horatio Seymour.
1863-65. }
1855-57. Myron H. Clark.
1857-59. John A. King.
1859-63. Edwin D. Morgan.
1865-69. Reuben E. Fenton.
1873-75. John A. Dix.
1875-77. Samuel J. Tilden.
1877-80. Lucius Robinson.
1880-83 Alonzo B. Cornell.
1883. Grover Cleveland,

To these may be added the following Lieut. Governors, some of whom have national fame:—Erastus Root, Daniel S. Dickinson, George W. Patterson, Sanford E. Church, Henry J. Raymond, Stewart L. Woodford, Thomas G.

Alvord, Allen C. Beach, John C. Robinson, and George G. Hoskins.

LAWYERS.

Among the illustrious names that have reflected brightness on the escutcheon of the Empire State, are the following eminent jurists, most of whom have made themselves felt in the institutions of this city.

James Kent.
Reuben H. Walworth.
Ambrose Spencer.
Sanford E. Church.
William F. Allen.
Charles J. Folger.

All strongly marked by the true New England character in which they had a birthright. To these we add the names of the scarcely less distinguished Lyman Tremain, Ira Harris, Amasa J. Parker, Rufus W. Peckham, and William L. Learned, long residents of Albany.

In making the following lists, we may be guilty of errors of omission and commission; but have been guided by the best authorities we could obtain. We trust the errors are very few.

NEW ENGLAND LAWYERS IN ALBANY, NOW DECEASED.

Otis Allen.
Le Grand Bancroft.
Ebenezer Baldwin.
Daniel D. Barnard.

Isaac Edwards.
James Edwards.
Azariah C. Flagg.
Ebenezer Foote.

Lewis Benedict, Jr.
Nathaniel S. Benton.
Alexander W. Bradford.
Greene C. Bronson.
Aaron Burr.
Benjamin F. Butler.
Clarke B. Cochran.
Samuel G. Courtney.
T. Le Roy Case.
Amos Dean.
George Dexter.
James Dexter.
John A. Dix.
John Lovett.
Cicero Loveridge.
William L. Marcy.
William S. Paddock.
Matthew Patten.
Geo. W. Peckham.
Rufus W. Peckham.
John H. Reynolds.
Marcus T. Reynolds.
Theodore Sedgwick.
A. C. Southwick.
Ambrose Spencer.
John C. Spencer.
Samuel Stevens.

Samuel A. Foote.
W. W. Frothingham.
John Gould.
Isaac Hamilton.
Jabez D. Hammond.
Ira Harris.
F. II. Hastings.
Gideon Hawley.
Nicholas Hill.
Samuel M. Hopkins.
Lemuel Jenkins.
James Kent.
Hale Kingsley.
Alfred B. Street.
Richard M. Strong.
J. B. Sturtevant.
Azor Taber.
Grenville Tremain.
Lyman Tremain.
Reuben H. Walworth.
Henry G. Wheaton.
James M. Whelpley.
Elisha Williams.
Gilbert L. Wilson.
John Q. Wilson.
George Wolford.
Deodatus Wright.

LAWYERS OF NEW ENGLAND ANCESTRY,

WHO NOW ARE OR HAVE BEEN IN PRACTICE IN ALBANY.

Buel C. Andrews.
William Barnes.
John M. Bailey.
Alpheus T. Bulkley.
Isaac B. Barrett.
Eugene Burlingame.
Alden Chester.
Andrew J. Colvin.
Philander Deming.
Andrew S. Draper.
W. Frothingham.
W. D. Frothingham.
Scott D'M. Goodwin.
Matthew Hale.
William H. Hale.
Lewis B. Hall.
Stephen H. Hammond.
Hamilton Harris.
Frederick Harris.
Henry Q. Hawley.
Nathan Hawley.
Galen R. Hitt.
Charles M. Jenkins.
John M. Kimball.
J. Howard King.
Dwight King.
Isaac Lawson.
Joseph M. Lawson.
Wm. L. Learned.

Henry S. McCall.
Henry S. McCall, Jr.
Charles W. Mead.
Nathaniel C. Moak.
Edward Newcomb.
John T. Norton.
John J. Olcott.
John K. Porter.
Amasa J. Parker.
Amasa J. Parker Jr.
Rufus W. Peckham, Jr.
William F. Rathbone.
William P. Rudd.
Joseph W. Russell.
Edward Savage.
O. H. Shepard.
S. O. Shepard.
Henry Smith.
Horace E. Smith.
Geo. L. Stedman.
Benjamin I. Stanton.
Alvah H. Tremain.
Edward Wade.
Hiram L. Washburn.
William G. Weed.
Robert H. Wells.
Bradford R. Wood.
J. Hampden Wood.
Geo. M. Wright.

PHYSICIANS.

In the profession of medicine Albany has many names of men who have adorned the city by their talents, and helped it on in some of its most valued institutions, especially its Medical Schools and Hospitals. Among the most illustrious, New England has contributed Drs. Tully, Stearns, Willard, Wing, Cogswell, Bigelow, March, Armsby and others, who have yielded to that conqueror whose weapons their skill often parried, but who subdues all at last. They have left names long held dear alike in the cottages of the humble and in the mansions of the rich and learned.

The following is a list of the physicians of this city now deceased, who sprang from New England stock, followed by the names of those now living :—

James H. Armsby.
Geo. H. Armsby.
James L. Babcock.
James S. Bailey.
Uriah G. Bigelow.
Asa Burbank.
Moses F. Clement.
Mason F. Cogswell.
Charles D. Cooper
Palmer C. Dorr
Harris I. Fello
Edward W. Ford.
Henry Green.
Henry R. Haskins.
J. Warren Hinckley.
Carroll Humphrey.
Wm. Humphrey.

John James.
Otis Jenks.
Jonathan Johnson.
Zina W. Lay.
Edward A. Leonard.
Enoch Leonard.
Solomon Lincoln.
Alden March.
vi Moore.
rd A. Munson.
Chas. A. Robertson.
John Stearns.
John H. Trotter.
William Tully.
Ashbel S. Webster.
Elias Willard.
Sylvester D. Willard.

Isaac Hyde.   Erastus Williams.
Daniel James.   Platt Williams.
Edwin James.   Joel A. Wing.

NOW LIVING.

Wm. H. Bailey.   C. S. Merrill.
Lewis Balch.   Wm. H. Murray.
James F. Barker.   Geo. H. Newcomb.
John M. Bigelow.   M. R. C. Peck.
Frederick C. Curtis.   Charles H. Porter.
Charles Devol.   Timothy K. Perry.
Amos Fowler.   Norman L. Snow.
Samuel H. Freeman.   George T. Stevens.
Lorenzo Hale.   Willis G. Tucker.
Henry March.   Samuel B. Ward.

TEACHERS.

Among the best gifts to Albany from New England are
some of its most useful and honored teachers. The Boys'
Academy has had Beck of perennial fame, Wood, Gates, and,
it is presumed, several others; the Girls' Academy, Booth,
Crittenden, Parsons and Stearns, and now the very worthy
Miss Plympton; the Normal School, Page, Perkins, Cochrane,
Woolworth, Alden, and just now, Waterbury, besides many
most useful male and female assistants; the High School now
has John E. Bradley, Oscar D. Robinson, Charles A. Horne,
Austin Sanford and Richard Prescott; the Grammar grades
have had, or now have Valentine, Bulkley, Gilbert, Howe,
Cass, Packer, and probably many others both male and female,
whose records we have not yet been able to secure.

Besides these, the Schools of Law and Medicine were founded and have been manned almost entirely by men of New England birth or antecedents, as shown elsewhere.

It should be added, that the present Superintendent of Schools is Charles W. Cole, son of that venerable man, so long useful to this city in the cause of education and public justice, John Orton Cole, a native of Connecticut.

AUTHORS.

Albany has not had many of the class of writers who give their whole time and talent to authorship. It is true that many excellent things have been written here, outside of journalism and the pulpit, which have had a wide and influential admiration. Some have been very effective, as intended, in promoting good morals, education and public improvements of many kinds; and have thus had a lasting influence. But most of our best known writers have written amid the pressure of professional duties, and as the outcome of professional study, that they might enlarge their sphere of active good. Among our most prolific authors may be named the following: Among the clergy, Sprague, Palmer and Clarke; among the lawyers, Kent, Walworth, Edwards, Dean, McCall and Moak; among the physicians, Tully, March and Willard; among educators, Page, Alden, Perkins, Davies; among scientists, T. R. and L. C. Beck, Hall and Emmons; among the poets, Street and Saxe; and Southwick, Buel, Croswell and Munsell, on more miscellaneous themes. All these claimed a New England birthright.

ORATORS.

Our practical people are not given to oratory; they speak by their deeds. But all admire the orator they cannot imitate. Such men crop out now and then among our lawyers and divines, and sometimes where we least look for them, among our men of affairs and our toiling men. Daniel D. Barnard was always listened to with pleasure; so was Henry G. Wheaton; Lyman Tremain was a man of eloquence, something of the Rufus Choate order. Albany never had a man that would excite his audience with his uncultivated yet electric eloquence, like the rough carpenter, James Kilburn. Among our divines, with differing graces of oratory,—persuasive, convincing, moving, pleasing, magnetic or powerful,—we may name, without question, as ranking very high in pulpit oratory, Eliphalet Nott, John M. Bradford, John Chester, Hooper Cumming, Bartholomew T. Welch, Wm. B. Sprague, Edward N. Kirk, Orville Dewey and Elias L. Magoon,—all the gift of New England. To these should be added the names of men whose preeminent statesmanship has, each in its time and manner, done so much, not only for the good of this city, but for the whole nation. Wm. L. Marcy, Silas Wright, John C. Spencer, Benj. F. Butler, John A. Dix, Daniel D. Barnard and Bradford R. Wood belong to this class. They all took pride in their New England blood, and made Albany. at least some part of their lives, their home.

BOOKS AND LECTURES.

Albany has, also, been swayed by such gifted thinkers and orators from New England as Daniel Webster, Wendell Phillips, Edward Everett, Ralph Waldo Emerson, Edwin P. Whipple, John B. Gough, Theodore Parker, Oliver Wendell Holmes, Charles Sumner, Thomas Starr King, and most others of its leading platform lecturers.

Their influence has been felt here; it has impressed itself on many minds and led to better lives and nobler deeds. Should it not be placed to the credit of New England in Albany?

And who writes the books our children use in the Sabbath and Day Schools? Who the books and periodicals that delight our hours of leisure, rest us when we are weary, instruct us when we are ignorant, uplift us when we are depressed and urge us on when we are faltering in life's journey? Are they not, most of them, from the homes of New England?

JOURNALISM AND JOURNALISTS.

In this department of quiet yet mighty energy, New England has given to Albany its full share. Among them we have only to name Charles R. Webster, that early printer, who so long gave the people knowledge in city and in country, a sort of *vox clamantis in deserto*, aiming to be successful only as he was true to the interests of the people; the earnest, ambitious Solomon Southwick, who grew better and better as long as he lived; the wise and useful Jesse Buel and Luther Tucker; the keen Edwin Croswell, who wrote so potently and so gracefully; the ever diligent and practical Joel Munsell; and the master magician, Thurlow Weed, who was mighty in council, and carried to the editor's sanctum a clear head, a strong arm and a cogent pen. Sharper and mightier than swords were their pens; as long as New York State has a name their names will be respected.

ART AND ARTISTS.

At one time Albany had a "Gallery of Fine Arts," where were collected quite a display of good pictures by such artists as Durand, Sully, Peale, Chapman, Carleton, Weir, the Harts, Ames and others. But most of the artists sought more favored homes and the treasures of the gallery were scattered. Ames, who was the founder and leading spirit, had died. There are good pictures in Albany now in private homes, and some considerable art appreciation; but no organized exhibition or encouragement. Page, the younger Ames, the younger Palmer, Low, all of New England stock, were born here. Boughton once resided and now has family friends here. Launt Thompson was brought out here by Dr. Armsby. Wm. M. Hunt, born in Vermont, has left one of his masterpieces in our new capitol. Palmer has done some of the best work in American sculpture; while Elliot was a master in portrait painting; and Twitchell, many think, quite equals, if he does not excel him in some of the requisites of true portraiture.

ARCHITECTS AND BUILDERS.

The most noted of this class in the early part of this century were, Christopher Batterman of Boston, Philip Hooker and Elias Putnam of Connecticut, and Jonathan Lyman of Massachusetts. They designed and erected most of the larger and better public and private buildings of their time, which are still admired for the common sense of their proportions and the good taste and good finish of their work. They have stood well the test of time.

carried on by him. His sons, John B. member of the state senate, (Williams, 1869,) and George H., are now the active members of the firm. Mr. T. has long been prominent in business circles; is now Vice President of the 1st National Bank. He has held the office of Mayor four terms, 1860, '66, '70 and '72. He is a man of positive convictions, and bold in standing by them. This is shown by his official career in such notable and well-remembered instances as taking decided ground in favor of free speech, when some of the leaders of his political party endeavored, by a mob, to prevent an abolition convention in the city, just before the war: he going into the hall with the speakers, and enforcing order; also, in the Dudley Observatory controversy and in the High School question. He has been a presidential elector.

Isaiah Townsend came to Albany in 1799; b. Orange Co.; d. Feb. 17, 1838, aged 61. For 36 years, he was engaged in an extensive and active manufacturing and mercantile business, in company with his brother, John Townsend. The house was very enterprising and liberal, and did much to advance the interests of this city. It was known, indeed, all over the country, as honorable, skillful and just. Gen. Frederick Townsend, Gen. Franklin Townsend, Theodore Townsend, Rufus K. Townsend, Dr. Franklin Townsend, and the late Dr. Howard Townsend, all honored and valuable citizens, are descendants of these men. Their ancestors were from Rhode Island.

John Townsend, b. Stirling Iron Works, June 14, 1783; came to Albany, 1802, and joined his brother Isaiah, in the hardware and iron foundry business, in which they successfully continued many years. Was 6 years Mayor of A.; d. Albany, Aug. 26, 1854. He was one of the founders of the

Syracuse Coarse Salt Co., of which he was president; was president, also, of Commercial Bank, of Exchange Bank, of Savings Bank, and an officer of many other organizations of business enterprise and public good.

Franklin Townsend, s. of Isaiah, b. Albany; has been Adjutant General of the State, and president of State Bank; was Mayor of the city, 1850. Gen. Frederick Townsend is a brother, and Dr. Franklin, Jr., a son.

Lyman Tremain, b. Durham, N. Y., June 14, 1819; d. New York, Nov. 30, 1878. His ancestors were from Berkshire Co., Mass. Studied and practiced law in his native town, until he came to A., in 1853, where he had his home, and pursued his brilliant career as a lawyer, until his death. He was among the foremost in his profession; eminent as a jury lawyer; electric as an orator on the platform, or anywhere. He served as District Attorney 2 years, and County Judge 4 years, in Greene Co.; as member of Assembly from Albany, and Speaker of that body, in 1866; as Attorney General of the State two years; and as Congressman-at-large from the State, 1873-5. He was candidate for Lt. Governor in 1862. Until 1861, he was a Democrat; after this he acted with the Republican party. His exalted patriotism, and burning eloquence were called into active service during the late civil war. His son, Col. Frederick, died of wounds in the service; and Grenville, another son, a lawyer of splendid promise, died just before his father.

Luther Tucker, b. Brandon, Vt., 1802; d. Albany, Jan. 26, 1873. A printer; in 1826, established the first daily paper west of Albany, at Rochester, and called it the "*Daily Advertiser*;" then started that pioneer agricultural journal, the

HOTELS.

The representative taverns, inns, coffee houses, tontines, hotels, and such like, have usually been kept, each in its way, by " the right man in the right place ;" among them Robert Lewis, Leverett Crittenden, Christopher Dunn, Ananias Platt, Matthew Gregory and Charles E. Leland, all from New England. To these men is greatly due the fact that Albany has, for three-quarters of a century, always had first-class public houses.

BANKS AND BANKERS.

It is claimed that the first movement for a Bank in this city was made by Elkanah Watson about 1791. It was the "Old Albany " put into operation in 1792 ; the second in New York and the fourth in the United States. It continued until 1861. It was opposed at first as needless and hazardous. When the books were opened, the whole amount of stock was taken in less than three hours. Watson was one of the first directors of this bank and also of the "State", which started in 1803. Of this latter bank, Rufus H. King was president nearly thirty years, succeeded by his son-in-law, Franklin Townsend, and his son, J. Howard King. The Mechanics and Farmers came next, in 1811, and was under the direction of Solomon Southwick, Benjamin Knower, Elisha Dorr, Isaac Hutton and others. G. A. Worth was cashier. Thomas W. Olcott was, for many years, its president, succeeded by his son, Dudley Olcott. It has always had its full share of public confidence ; its managers and stockholders have been largely New England men. No bankers in the United States have enjoyed a better reputation for financial sagacity and integrity than Rufus H. King, Thomas W. Olcott and Chauncey P. Williams. To-day, all the Banks of Albany stand on the surest foundation and are universally trusted. A list of those which have presidents of New England birth or ancestry, with their names, is herewith given :—

Matthew II. Read, First National.
Billings P. Learned, Union.
Chauncey P. Williams, Exchange.
William G. Thomas, Exchange Savings.
J. Wilbur Tillinghast, Merchants.
J. Howard King, State.
Dudley Olcott, Mechanics and Farmers.
Erastus Corning, City.
Benj. W. Wooster, County.

MERCHANTS, MANUFACTURERS AND OTHER BUSINESS MEN.

In a city so well situated by nature for trade, and, in later times aided by art, there has been always, for an inland town, a large proportion of traders and merchants, representing nearly every class of trade. Many of them have made their own goods ; or commencing as mechanics and manufacturers, have gone, in riper years and with the gains of prosperity, into trade. The usual ups and downs of mercantile life have been seen and felt here. A complete list of those thus engaged, it would be impossible to present in this essay. They have represented all nations and people. Among the most prosperous have been Erastus Corning, Rufus H. King, Isaiah and John Townsend, Matthew and Samuel Patten, Friend Humphrey, James Goold, and, in more recent or present

Genesee Farmer, in 1831 ; this he afterwards consolidated with the *Cultivator* of Jesse Buel, in Albany. In 1852, he started the *Country Gentleman*, which is still continued by his sons, Luther H. and Gilbert M. Tucker, with marked ability, and a very large circulation. Dr. Willis G. Tucker, one of the Faculty of the Medical College, and of the College of Pharmacy, is also a son.

Wm. Tully, b. Saybrook Point, Conn., Feb. 18, 1785; d. Springfield, Mass., Feb. 28, 1859; gr. Yale, 1806; practiced medicine with Dr. March in Albany, 1826, and a few years later. Was regarded by many as the most learned and scientific physician of his time. Was a great student, an able lecturer, a vigorous writer. His views were positive, his prejudices strong, his criticisms caustic, his attacks upon what he deemed errors, merciless. As a practitioner, he was heroic, allowing no questioning as to his treatment. His numerous contributions to the literature of medicine, abating something for minuteness of detail or diffuseness, were greatly esteemed. His reputation as a medical writer rests chiefly on his great work " Materia Medica, or Pharmacology and Therapeutics," 2 vols. His lectures were given at Castleton, in South Carolina, and Yale (1829-41.)

Asa W. Twitchell, b. Swanzey, N. H., Jan. 1, 1820; came to Lansingburgh, N. Y. 1834; to Albany, 1843. He painted his first portrait in 1839; recently spent a few months among the galleries of Europe; has painted many of the best portraits of the city; holds a first class rank as an artist; is especially happy in presenting his subject, not as a picture, but as a character in active business or professional life. He is still, daily, in his studio, doing work that will long do him honor.

Thomas W. Valentine, b. Norton, Mass., Feb. 16, 1818; d. Brooklyn, N. Y., April 4, 1879; from 1842–53, was principal of a Public School in Albany; went to Brooklyn in 1855. While in A. he was for a while Superintendent of the Albany Orphan Asylum and Editor of the New York Teacher. In 1857 he was president of the New York State Teachers' Association, and made the first movement toward the establishment of the National Education Association of the United States. He was a man of retiring habits, but of earnest purpose and broad views. The State of New York owes him gratitude for efficient aid in building up its present system of public education.

Franklin Vose, b. Spencer, N. Y., 1822: came to Albany in 1846, and Rodney, his brother, b. Spencer, 1824, came in 1849. Both became successful lumber merchants, Rodney still carrying on the business and ranking well among our many enterprising and prosperous lumber traders. He is descended from Robert, of Dorchester, Mass., and related to that distinguished educator of N. E., Hon. John Vose, of N. H.

Reuben H. Walworth, b. Bozrah, Conn., Sept. 26, 1788; d. Saratoga, Nov. 26, 1866; spent his early years in Hoosick, N. Y., where his father moved in 1793; was admitted to the bar at Troy, 1809; practiced some years at Plattsburg: was active in the war of 1812; M. C. 1821–23; Chancellor of the State, 1828 to '48, during a part of which time he resided in Albany. He was pronounced by Judge Story, " the greatest Equity jurist living." He was a man of large benevolence, and a firm and active friend of temperance and religion. Rev. Clarence A. Walworth, rector of St. Mary's, Albany, since 1866; gr. Union, 1838; a devoted priest. a useful citizen, a scholar and a writer, is a son.

times, George C. Treadwell, Newton & Co,, Bacon, Stickney
& Co., E. P. Durant, Weare C. Little, E. J. Larrabee, E. A.
Hobbs, John S. Perry & Co., D. G. Littlefield, Rathbone,
Sard & Co., Weed, Parsons & Co., Wm. M. Whitney & Co..
Henry Russell, Geo. H. Thacher & Son, Kibbee & Dalton,
B. W. Wooster, S. L. Munson, Mather Brothers, J. Benedict
& Son, R. W. Thacher, James W. Eaton, C. W. Eaton, G.
W. Luther, G. B. Hoyt, D. S. Lathrop, T. C. Cooper, Moore
& Bellows, Justus F. Taylor, Judson & Capron, Jesse C. Potts,
Paul Cushman, Alexander Gregory, and others of the New
England class of Manufacturers and Merchants.

BIOGRAPHICAL NOTES.

Joseph Alden, b. Cairo, N. Y., Jan. 4, 1807; descendant of
John Alden of the Mayflower; gr. Union, 1829; D. D. Union
1838; LL. D., Columbia, 1857. Studied Theology at Princeton; tutor there two years. Ordained pastor of Congregation-
alist Church, Williamstown, Mass., 1834; prof. Williams,
1835- 52; prof. moral philos., Lafayette, 1852- 7: pres.. Jefferson, 1857- 67; pres. N. Y. State Normal School, Albany,
1867- 82. Author of many juvenile books, Elements of Intellectual Philosophy, Science of U. S. Government, Christian
Ethics, English Grammar, and a large contributor to N. Y.
Observer and other religious journals. William L. Alden, the
author, is a son.

Otis Allen, b. Surry, N. H., Oct. 15, 1804; d. Albany, Mar.
27, 1865; came to this city and became law partner of Israel
Williams, in 1833; of F. H. Hastings, until 1848; after this
was without partner. An accurate, honest, successful lawyer;
a citizen most heartily respected and trusted.

Ezra Ames, b. Mass. about 1768; was in Albany in 1793; d. Feb. 23, 1836, a. 68. He was a painter, and acquired distinction as a student of art; executed with great fidelity a large number of original portraits and made copies of many paintings of merit. He was a director in the Mechanics and Farmers' Bank, and left a good estate. Julius Rubens, an artist of promise, who died young, and Angelo, a well known resident of this city, are his sons.

James H. Armsby, b. Sutton, Mass., d. Albany, Dec. 3, 1875; succeeded Dr. March as professor of Anatomy and Physiology at Castleton, Vt., 1834; in 1838, resigned, and devoted nearly all his time to raising funds to furnish and fit up a Museum and other things necessary to the establishment of a Medical College in Albany. Of this college he was one of the founders and always a devoted friend. He was one of the most popular of its lecturers from the first. He was, also, one of the founders of the Albany Hospital and of the Dudley Observatory. Always a public spirited, large hearted citizen, intent upon doing good, especially to young men of talent and moral worth. He held many honorable official positions. A bronze bust has been placed in Washington Park, by his students, aided by citizens, to commemorate the deeds of this good physician and great public benefactor. Dr. Gideon H. Armsby was his son.

John F. Bacon, b. Mass., settled in Albany as a lawyer; Clerk of State Senate, 1814-40; was U. S. Consul at Nassau, N. P., about 10 years; d. there Feb. 25, 1860, a. 71.

Samuel N. Bacon, b. Harvard, Mass., Jan. 25, 1829; came to A. 1848, is senior member of the large, long established and prosperous Coffee and Spice Establishment of Bacon,

Stickney & Co., which grew out of the house of L. A. Chase & Co. Mr. C. was a native of Hillsborough, N. H.; d. 1857, leaving large wealth and an unblemished name, which their successors have fully sustained.

Daniel D. Barnard, b. Sheffield, Mass., 1797; d. Albany, Apr. 24, 1861; gr. Williams, 1818; began law practice at Rochester, N. Y., 1821; came to Albany 1832; was member of Assembly; M. C. 1828–30 and 1839–45; Minister to Prussia 1849–53; an active whig politician; a vigorous writer for *Whig Review* and other periodicals; a popular orator; published many addresses. LL. D., Geneva.

Ezra A. Bartlett, descended from Dr. Josiah Bartlett of N. H., one of the signers of the Declaration of Independence, and belongs to a family noted for physicians of eminence; b. Newouryport, Mass., July 18, 1845; gr. Rochester University; gr. M. D., Albany Medical College, and is now a lecturer in the College and a resident physician.

Lewis C. Beck, b. Schenectady, N. Y., Oct. 4, 1798; d. Albany, Apr. 21, 1853; gr. Union, 1817; brother of Dr. T. R. Beck. Came to Albany, about 1821; gave lectures and lessons in botany and chemistry in Rensselaer Institute, Vt. Academy of Medicine, and Middlebury College; in 1827, took charge of the New York Mineral Survey; in 1830, was prof. of Chemistry and Natural History at Rutgers. At time of his death, was prof. of Chemistry in Albany Medical College. His published scientific writings are numerous and valuable.

Theodoric Romeyn Beck, of New England Ancestry, "his ancestors being among the first settlers of New England," b. Schenectady, N. Y., Aug. 11, 1791; d, Utica, Nov. 19, 1855; began to practice medicine in Albany, 1813; was principal of

Albany Academy from 1817–48, in which position he gained a great reputation as an educator and left a lasting influence for good on the young men of Albany. While in this position, and during the few remaining years of his life, he did much collateral, useful and scholarly work, which places him high among the benefactors and scholars of our country. He gave lectures at Albany Medical College, 1840–54; was pres. State Medical Society, 1829; manager of the State Lunatic Asylum; founder of the Albany Institute, some years its president and promoter of its best working plans; for many years editor the *Am. Journal of Insanity*; published many valuable papers, addresses and reports. His famous work on "Medical Jurisprudence" is standard in Europe as well as in America and has given him the name of father of that Science. In philanthrophic works, his head, heart and hand were all in them.

Lewis Benedict. of Mass. stock: b. Albany Sept. 2, 1817; killed in battle at Pleasant Hill, La., April 9, 1864; gr. Williams, 1837; began practice of law, 1841; held offices of City Attorney; Judge Advocate; and Surrogate of Albany Co., 1848 –52; also Memb. of Assembly, 1860. Went into the Union service in 1861, as Lt. Col., and was conspicuous for soldierly conduct and bravery until he fell leading a charge. Became Col. and then brevet Brig. Gen. The G. A. R. Lew Benedict Post, was named in honor of him.

Uriah G. Bigelow, belonging to a family remarkable for producing many eminent physicians, originating in Mass., or now residing there; was b. Worcester, N. Y., Oct. 21, 1821; practiced medicine, with marked success in Albany, about 30 years; d. Feb. 23, 1873.

John M. Bigelow, son of Dr. Uriah G., b. Albany, August

Samuel B. Ward, son of D. B. and Abby Dwight Partridge of Mass.; b. New York, July 8, 1842; gr. Columbia. Since he came to Albany, he has held a leading place among its eminent physicians and surgeons, and is a member of the faculty of the Medical College.

Edward P. Waterbury, b. Franklin. N. Y,, May 10, 1831; gr. Albany Normal School; teacher for 13 years, in Albany Academy, and 14 years agent of Mass. Life Ins. Co. Was appointed principal of Albany Normal School to succeed Rev. Dr. Alden, in 1882.

Elkanah Watson, b. Plymouth, Mass., Jan. 22, 1758; d. Port Kent, N. Y., Dec. 5, 1842. In 1773, was a merchant's clerk in Providence; executed important commercial trusts during the revolution; in 1779, bore despatches to Franklin, at Paris; for 3 years, engaged in commerce at Nantes; then visited England, Holland and Flanders; returned to Newport, R. I., and from thence went to Albany in 1789, where, for 18 years, he was an active promoter of public enterprises. From 1807–16, resided in Pittsfield, Mass., where he devoted himself to agriculture; founded Berkshire Agric. Soc.; returned to Albany in 1816, and founded first Agricultural Society in the State of New York; made a tour of Michigan and the Lakes, round by Montreal, with reference to better facilities for trading western products, in New York and Boston; made the first suggestions in regard to the canal improvements that were carried out and completed by De Witt Clinton in the N. Y. and Erie Canal, in 1824; went to Port Kent in 1828. His numerous notes of travel; his essays on agriculture and other public matters; his activity in promoting public enterprises, entitle him to a large place in the list of our nation's benefactors. Albany owes him much.

John H. Webb, partner of George Dummer in 1807, afterwards associated with him H. L. Webb, and continued, until 1829. He d. in Hartford, Conn., Sept.14, 1847. The house continued under the name of H. L. and C. B. Webb until 1844, when it sold out to Gregory & Co. It was the first house in this business that extended its trade to the then far off wilderness of the North West Territory. They established in 1834, a branch at Detroit. *H. L. Webb* was active in founding the Canal Bank, and was president of the Gas Light Company. He died in Hartford, Conn., Oct 1846.

Charles R. Webster, b. Hartford, Conn., Sept. 30, 1762; d. Saratoga Springs, July 18, 1834; printer; came to Albany in 1781, and went on a small weekly paper with S. Balantine. In 1784, he started the *Albany Gazette*, which continued under his guidance, the leading paper of the city for about 40 years, and existed until 1845. In the capacity of leading journalist, conspicuous for a ready enterprise, a broad public spirit, a liberal philanthropy, and discriminating charity, he, more, perhaps, than any other citizen of his time, became identified with the leading interests of the city, and promoted its prosperity. Bookselling, binding and publishing became a part of his business. He pub. the *Daily Advertiser* in addition to his weekly. His twin bro. George, and his nephews, Elisha W., Hezekiah and Daniel Skinner, became partners before 1800. Their *Gazette* was widely circulated over the then new settlements of the State west of the Hudson River. He was very active in all efforts to encourage young mechanics, and excite in them intelligence and self-respect. To this end, he joined in the formation of the Mechanics' Society, which was largely officered and carried on by mechanics from the common schools of New England, and was a power for good many years.

Thurlow Weed; father from Stamford, Conn.; b. Catskill, N. Y., Nov. 15, 1797; d. New York City, Nov. 22, 1882; became a printer; in 1826-7, edited the *Anti-Masonic Enquirer*; elected twice to the State Assembly; came to Albany in 1830 as Editor of the *Albany Journal*, and continued until 1862, gaining an immense power as a journalist and party leader, and holding it many years. While declining all public offices himself, he was largely instrumental in bringing forward such men as Harrison, Taylor, Scott, Seward and others. He was wise in council and powerful in action, and ranks with Greeley and a few others as one of the greatest journalists of his time. His pen was always busy in notes of travel, reminiscences, and political counsel after he retired from his editorial chair, which might be called the Chair of State, so potent was his influence. Of course, such a man was largely influential in shaping affairs in this city. His daughter Emily is wife of Hon. William Barnes, and mother of Thurlow Weed Barnes.

Bartholomew T. Welch, b. Boston, Sept. 24, 1794: d. Newtonville, N. Y., Dec. 9, 1870; entered ministry in 1824; pastor of Baptist Church, now called Emmanuel, 1828-48; a preacher of great eloquence and power; very active in public enterprises; first excited public attention to the need of a public cemetery, in a sermon preached Dec. 1840, which led to the opening of that beautiful city of the loved and departed, the Rural Cemetery, consecrated to its sacred uses in 1844.

Elias Willard, b. Harvard, Mass., Jan. 7, 1756; d. Albany, Mar. 20, 1837. He was at the battle of Lexington, April 19, 1775, and served as military surgeon during the revolutionary war. Came to Stillwater, N. Y., 1785, and to Albany, 1801, where, for 25 years, he was extensively engaged in the practice of medicine and surgery. Patient, diligent, devoted to his work. a sincere christian, a noble patriot, ever ready to do good. he was beloved, and, in his last years, venerated. *Dr. Moses*, his brother, prominent in his profession, practiced here a few years and went to New York in 1821. Dr. E. W. Ford, and Dr. John H. Trotter, his grandsons, practiced later in this city.

Sylvester D. Willard, b. Wilton, Conn , June 19, 1825 ; d. Albany, Apr. 2, 1865 ; came to Albany in 1845 ; gr. Alb. Med. Col., and began practice in 1848. Ever after, while not regardless of the daily calls of his profession, he devoted much time to its local history and the biography of deceased physicians, the results of which appear in "Albany Medical Annals, Vol.1." He also did service as a Volunteer Surgeon in 1862, and successfully interested himself in securing state aid for the relief of sick and wounded soldiers. His crowning acts relate to his agency in ascertaining the condition of the insane poor of the State, which led to the establishment of the "Willard Asylum for the Insane, " so named as a memorial of him since his decease   At the time of his death he was holding the position of Secretary of the State Medical Society, examining Surgeon for the Pension office, and Surgeon General of the State, all of which were to him posts of arduous labor and unceasing fidelity.

Chauncey P. Williams, b. Middletown, Conn., 1817 ; came to Albany in 1835, and successfully followed the lumber trade for 25 years. Was a director of the Albany Exchange Bank, and its president in 1856. In 1861, entered upon the business of banking as a profession, and has ever since followed it in this same bank, first as cashier and then again as president. Through the recent civil war, this bank, under his management, had the agency, in this vicinity, for obtaining loans for the U. S. government, which was carried on skillfully in the spirit of wise finance as well as good patriotism, and aided much the Government credit. Mr. W. was one of the founders, and is a leading supporter of the Congregational Church.

James Wilson, b. Londonderry, N. H., 1763; d. Mar. 26, 1855, in Bradford, Vt., where he had owned a farm since 1796, and resided when not engaged in his globe manufacture. He was from his boyhood, fond of mathematics, geography and astronomy, and made a celestial and a terrestrial globe, the first ever made in this country and presented them to the city of Boston in 1814. In 1815, he established the first Globe manufactory in the United States, at Albany, assisted by his sons Samuel and John, and continued the work successfully, with great credit, making many improvements, until the death of his sons. He did his own designing and engraving.

Joel A. Wing, b. Berkshire Co., Mass.. Aug. 13, 1788; d. Hartford, Conn., Sept. 6, 1852. Spent his professional life as physician in Albany ever after 1814; president of Co. and State Med. Societies. With a wonderfully retentive memory and eager fondness for knowledge, his medical attainments were very extensive; his practice was very large and his counsel frequently sought. Few physicians ever excelled him in acuteness of perception or prompt action in treatment of a case; few were more welcome in the sick room or more highly esteemed by all classes of society.

Bradford R. Wood, b. Westport, Conn., Sept. 30, 1800; gr. Union, 1824; came to Albany 1824; read law and has practiced his profession here ever since, taking an active interest in public affairs, and in the civil, intellectual and moral advancement of the city. He was M. C. 1845-47, where his action was independent, above party, statesmanlike. He was subsequently U. S. Minister to Denmark. He was one of the founders and is a leading supporter of the Congregational Church in this city. Gen. J. Hampden Wood, is a son.

Darius S. Wood, b. Westboro, Mass., July 1821; became an engineer at B. & W. R. Rd. shops; ran the first passenger train into Albany on the B. & A. R. Rd.; held important trusts as engineer at Niagara Falls and W. Albany; was very skillful, and patented many valuable car improvements; d. Albany, Feb. 1881.

Royal Woodward, b. Ashford, Conn., Nov. 13, 1815; d. Albany, Oct. 2, 1882; silk manufacturer and merchant; had resided in A. many years; a very estimable man; intelligent and unostentatious. Had collected a library of about 30,000 volumes, probably the largest private library in the country, outside of New York City.

Samuel B. Woolworth, b. Bridgehampton, L. I., Dec. 15, 1800; gr. Hamilton, 1822; was successively teacher in Academies of Monson, Mass., Onondaga and Homer, N. Y., until 1852; was principal of Albany Normal School, 1852–56; and Secretary of Board of Regents 1856, to 1880. In all these positions he was a faithful, efficient, conscientious educator, and did vast good. He served as trustee of Hamilton College 44 years; was one of the founders and a president of the N. Y. State Teachers' Association. His ancestors were from New England.

Gorham A. Worth, b. Nantucket, about 1773; his father came to Hudson, N. Y., and taught school. He came to Albany as teller in New York State Bank, in 1803, and became first Cashier of Mechanics and Farmers' Bank, in

1811; had charge of United States Branch Bank, at Cincinnati, 1817–21; removed to New York; for many years president of City Bank of N. Y.; acquired wealth and high social position there. Was an intelligent observer and a ready writer. Wrote "*Recollections of Albany*," and *Reminiscences of Cincinnati*;" d. New Orleans, Apr. 3, 1856, aged 73.

CONCLUSION.

Thus have we completed the task of selecting from the history of this city, matters that relate to a class of men who began to come here from New England about 100 years ago. We have tried to gather up the names of the earliest of them; to show the condition of society and affairs when they came here, and what changes they inaugurated. We have detailed some of the leading enterprises in which they engaged, and some of the results, as they have been brought about by the continued efforts of those who followed them with the advantages of more time, more light, more means, and larger opportunities. The task has been difficult because it required selection from a confused mass of unassorted history, most of it unwritten; afterwards to be arranged, compared, and condensed into the small space allowed by this paper.

We have added such antecedent and collateral history as seemed necessary to show how Albany has grown in a period of 260 years (1623– 1883) from a few miserable huts occupied by Holland fur traders to a city of 100,000 people, from every nation under heaven, busy with the hum of varied industry, possessing great wealth and all the elevating and refining advantages of modern civilization and growth. We have tried to be true to history, conscientiously faithful. Much has been left out because we could not, up to the time when our work must be completed, secure satisfactory knowledge; more, for the want of space in the limits assigned.

As a descendant of the Puritans we point with decent pride to the changes wrought. And yet we are not blind to the good work done by men with the blood of Holland, France, Germany, Scotland, Ireland and other nations, in their veins.

We are one now. Of one blood God hath made all people. We could select and write up the deeds and names of each with great satisfaction.

There is truth in the remark of Hon. Wm. L. Learned that "Albany was once a Dutch city; then it became a Yankee city; and now it is a city of all nations."

"He was of Puritan descent; his ancestors were noble ones; for the blood of the Pilgrims ran in their veins, and the love of the Pilgrim's God burned in their hearts." It was so said of one excellent man, who still has relatives in Albany. Well if it could be said of all of "Puritan descent," "that blood tells." Do all honor their birthright?

We should be glad if we could have presented what the New England women have done in Albany. If it could be told, we doubt not it would be a noble record That they are entitled to a full share of the credit given their fathers, husbands, brothers and sons, will not be denied. What a story theirs would make as mothers, wives and sisters,— a story of home fidelity, of loving entreaty, of wise counsel, of endurance borne, of christian grace, and of much public activity in works of benevolence and charity, in the name of learning and religion!

Says the late Hon. Lyman Tremain, one of Albany's most valued citizens, in a speech made at the Lyman Reunion in 1871, "It has been related of a prominent Ohio politician, who had thoughtlessly repeated the outcry against New England, that, when he came to look around him, and consider the elements of which the community was composed; and when he came to take out from among the people those who were born in New England, or were the descendants of New Englanders; those who married New England wives; or the children of New England parents; and, also, those who had been instructed by New England school-masters, or school mistresses; he found that those who were left would not amount to much; and so he concluded to say no more about " leaving New England out in the cold."